THE COBO
COFFEE CO.

HOPE UW ENJOY
THE RIDE... ,

CABO SAN LUCAS 2015

The names have been
changed to protect the
innocent, as well as the guilty

THE ESCAPE
TO CABO

S. A. LaPoint

I haven't any apologies for my Life

The decisions... whether wise or foolish, have thusly

defined the individual I am for eternity.

My regret is one...

The lost opportunity to be a Father & Grandfather

D & L... I love you very much

Before it all...

As far back as I can remember I have always had the desire to rob a bank, just turn the clocks back... 1880 will be just fine.

When asked "Scotty, what do you want to be when you grow up?"
My reply had always been... "I'm going to be a Bank Robber"
Grandpa Max called me his little "Jessie James"

In the first five years of my life it would be a rare occasion if you could catch me without my six-guns. My attire would not be complete without my strapping on the shiny black gun-belt trimmed with braided white leather... the home for my two hogs. It had plenty of loops for the lead, a lot were needed during those long distance shoot'em ups when I was trying to make my getaway. There were permanent indentions around both of my scrawny thighs where I had the holsters cinched down, should a fast draw be necessary.
Oddly enough, it was required more often than not.

One September morning, I had the horse saddled up and my sights on the next bank job. I was about to call the rest of the boys when Mrs. Frieze, the prettiest of the bank tellers, walked into the stables. There looked to be something mighty important on her mind...

"Scotty, honey... listen, we talked about this before, you know today is your first day of school. I will take good care of them while you're gone, you just can't take your pigs or whatever you call your play guns with you to the classroom"

Once I started attending school the hogs accompanied me less frequently... however, they were always in my adventure when the teachers caught me day dreaming.

While growing up with the normal trials and tribulations of life, my one burning desire never strayed far from my mind. When walking past a bank I would always imagine what it would be like to go in and rob it... like in the Old West.

In my early 20's I got a bartending job in a popular Southern California beach restaurant where I met a waitress named Janie. We were both hired on the same day and about to begin our seventh night shift together. When we met up in the parking lot she asked if she could hold on to my arm while she knocked the beach sand off of her sandals. Not the steadiest on only one of her bronzed to perfection sticks she almost brought us both down on the bed of ice plant that framed the Overlook Bar & Grill.

That would have been alright with me.

An off the charts head turner. Blond, tall, tan... a grill that lit up the room. Well complemented with all the trimmings. There wasn't any doubt that the Good Lord had allowed her to get into line twice. When she spoke it was so gentle and sweet you just waited for the honey to start dripping.

She also topped the charts in one other category... Coordination, she didn't have any... none, I'm talking zero-zilch-nada.

That's Janie.

You want to see something scary? Try watching that absolutely gorgeous creature walk over to a table with a full tray of drinks and attempt to lift one off… many a pissed off table of wet patrons, hell of a knee slap'n laughter fest for us admirers.
Her timid demeanor, sexy ass smile and genuine sweetness always seemed to extinguish the heat in short time.

One Monday evening, on attempt sixteen or so, she got the first three out of four drinks delivered without holding the tray with two hands, she didn't even ask the customer to lift his own drink off the tray. We were all watching, some with fingers crossed.

I kept one eye on Janie, the other on the hefty pile of wagers sitting on the bar. The bus boys were whispering, immediately a Regular got their attention and with the old finger across the throat signal… they quickly ceased.

KA-BAM… the tray hit the floor.

There were cheers from some and grumblings from others as the winnings were cut from the pile.

Janie came up the three stairs to the Overlook Bar, our perch where we got the bird's eye view of her deliveries. She had that ever so wonderful innocent look of youth and determination…

"I'm doing a lot better, I ALMOST did it!!!"
"I thought you had that one kid but hey, look on the bright side, nobody got wet!!"

She lit up and took off all wide eyed, in search of her next table of ~~victims~~ customers… obviously proud as hell with her progress.

Ok, I'm hooked… one hundred percent attracted to that uncoordinated, absolutely stunning, knock Scotty the hell over with a feather, wonderful, beautiful girl.

The manager had wanted to let her go a few times, but with the Regulars promising to boycott and/or burn down the joint with him in it if he did, he relented. My reasoning was more on a business level... the three nights a week that she worked, traditionally the slowest, had steadily been on the increase.

The wagering on her deliveries had become quite the attraction on Tuesday nights.

Janie and I had become inseparable. We marked our six month anniversary by toasting with a promise to continue our faithful bond for eternity.

That was a first for me.

I had made plans to move to Las Vegas before I met her. I didn't want to get into the comfort zone of bartending, which is easy to do with all the perks that go along with the job... especially in a tourist destination beach town.

I wanted to get into Real Estate. A friend had shared his opinions, predicting that the market in Nevada was about to explode...

"Las Vegas Scotty... you'll make a fortune"

I told Janie about my plans and with our love for each other in full bloom she wanted to go with me so we loaded up her silver 240 Z with all of our worldly possessions. Look out Vegas, here we come. In short time I grabbed a job bartending at a small casino and attended school at night for my license. Janie got a job at Bank of America as a teller.

I never told her about my Destiny.

At dinnertime I would enjoy her recounting of the daily events, in particular the safety meetings about what to do in case of a bank robbery. Not really believing that I would ever actually do it, the fantasy of bank robbery was deeply instilled and only enjoyed vicariously.

About a year later Janie and I tied the knot, The Little Chapel of the West. The ensuing two years produced unbelievably beautiful daughters, Dana and Lory.

Thank God they took after Mom.

With Real Estate license in hand I went to work with a purpose, achieving annual Top Sales position in my second year.

Everything was RIGHT, on top of the world and bullet proof.

Shortly after our third anniversary I came down with a severe case of Stupid.

It's an illness that normally affects young men in their late 20's or early 30's that feel that they have prematurely achieved success.
The symptoms range from an over inflated ego and selfishness to an exaggerated sense of self importance.
In its final stage... total memory loss of what's most important in life.

Janie discovered a miracle cure.

Once the divorce was final I felt the need to leave Las Vegas, my heart couldn't handle a chance encounter. Two weeks later I packed up my stuff... everything, including all the broken pieces that I could find from my self-inflicted broken heart. That proved to be a very difficult task; it had shattered into a million pieces.

My brother Tim owned several different car dealerships in Utah, New Mexico and Arizona. He offered me a chance to learn about the Automobile business and an opportunity to heal so I started working and learning the business at one of his dealerships in Salt Lake City.

Endeavoring into Auto Sales was good for me; a new challenge that kept my mind off my screwing up the greatest gift God gave to mankind… the opportunity to experience Love.

To say that I was able to keep my mind off the three greatest things in my life would be un-true, how about an eight hour reprieve with sixteen painful hours in between... no relief on weekends.

I quickly rose to the Sales Manager position. It didn't take me long to learn that Salt Lake City wasn't a great fit for me, so when an opportunity presented itself I transferred.

Santa Fe, New Mexico has its own heartbeat, the feel that heals all that ails you and the energy to set you back on your desired path.

It was what the doctor ordered.

After a year there and still fumbling for that comfort zone foothold in life my brother asked me to help out at his Toyota Store in Tucson.

Instant comfort zone, Arizona was where I wanted to live.

I transferred a week later.

Fourteen years blew by like the Supersonic Jets that practice in the limitless skies over Tucson on any given day and soon found myself nibbling on the big four-O.

I had a nice home in the Tucson foothills, good job, a new Lincoln and a Harley in the garage.

Why couldn't I get bank robbery off of my mind... for almost forty years?

The Banks

One beautiful Friday afternoon in Phoenix I had just finished a Seminar and was traveling on Camelback, a main east/west thoroughfare. The sunroof was open, the music selected was a fitting toast to the spectacular spring day. My mood couldn't have been better, things were clicking again. Upon arriving at the signal on 44th St. and while waiting for the light to change I glanced over and saw a Bank of America with a broad lawn. The landscaping was honed to perfection. It looked as though the various colors of the floral, the multiple shades of green in the lawn and trim, were actually pulsating…. glowing in the spring sunlight.

To the left of the bank was an office building with underground parking.

Exactly, what I had imagined throughout the years would make an ideal setting for a bank robbery.

I'm not quite sure if thought actually played a part, however I somehow maneuvered the necessary three lanes.

I found myself in the parking garage that was adjacent to the Bank, parked in a spot close to the middle on the ground floor.

I turned off the engine and leaned my head back on the soft leather of the headrest.

This has been on your mind for your entire life Scotty my boy, if you don't do it now, you never will.

I emptied the contents from my leather satchel that I had from my Seminar and on a blank piece of paper I wrote the note;

DO NOT TAKE YOUR EYES OFF THIS PIECE OF PAPER
DO <u>EXACTLY</u> AS YOU ARE TOLD

Walking through the garage towards the passageway to the bank I felt as if it were only a dream.

Autopilot had been clicked.

I was dressed like a typical Arizonan, maybe a Contractor… pressed Levi's, polished cowboy boots, starched long sleeve.

When I entered the bank I kept my eyes looking forward and on the floor. I looked up and to the right, quickly spotting a short hallway with a door marked Manager.

It was ajar so I tapped lightly and the manager looked up…

"May I help you?"

I stepped into his office…

"You sent me a letter and I wondered if you would clarify something for me"

He did an up & down quick scan review of me and probably determined a typical Arizona businessman stood before him, with satchel in hand, the type he would have sent a letter to.

"Yes, please, come in… what can I do for you?"

I kept my eyes on the floor as I walked to his desk and upon sitting down I placed the satchel on the floor to my side.

Continuing to keep my eyes cast downward I quickly opened it and grabbed the corner of the note with my fingernails. I made a grand loop to insure that the note dangling from my fingernails didn't arrive upside down. The action also served well as a method of diversion, it landed flush in front of the man, printed side up.

Once his eyes went to the note...

"Do NOT take your eyes off that piece of paper. Do <u>NOT</u> lift your eyes... DO YOU UNDERSTAND ME?"
"Yes"
"Call your assistant in here.... NOW"

He did as told, she quickly arrived.

"Please sit down next to me"

I then said to the manager...

"I need you to go into the vault and get me $100,000 dollars, there better not be any Dye-packs or Tracers because you and I are going to check when you get back and if there is... it will get real ugly in here. DO YOU UNDERSTAND ME?"
"Yes"
"You have 30 seconds to get back... GO"

He left for the vault, the young assistant was visibly shaken and I felt bad for putting her in this position...

"Listen... I am as scared as you are and I promise you no harm will come to you. I will be gone soon. I certainly hope you will receive some paid time off for this craziness, I am very sorry to put you through this"

The manager walked in and set a canvas bank bag in front of me.

"Is that the money?"
"Yes"
"Thank you very much"

I knew there would not be Dye-packs or Tracers. I paid attention to Janie's recounting on safety meetings, you say that you don't want em... liability dictates you don't get em.

Apparently someone in the Policy making department determined that it wasn't prudent to piss off the dude do'n the rob'n.

As I passed through the hallway and stepped into the lobby I couldn't seem to draw a breath, my heart was red lining and there was such a severe buzzing in my ears that all other sound was non-existent.

When the front doors opened I felt the strong flash of sunlight... the fresh air. Suddenly I was able to suck in a lung full, the buzz just abruptly stopped, like someone found the tripped breaker and flipped it back on.

All was functioning again.

It was frightening... it was exhilarating.

Walking with a purpose... not haste, I turned to the right, trying not to break into a run down the path to the parking garage.

For the past few seconds I had been waiting for someone to yell or the sound of an alarm to start blaring.

I can't believe I just did that. You're an IDIOT, I just robbed a goddamn bank!

As I entered the parking garage I could hear a bit of commotion behind me and then the alarm... My heart almost jumped out of my chest.

It took all the calm I could muster to not toss the satchel in the air and break into a panicked, free for all sprint to anywhere but there. When I rounded the wall to enter the garage I noticed a trash dumpster and upon dropping my satchel I ripped my shirt off, tossing it into the container.

Underneath my shirt I happened to be wearing a bright teal tank-top.

Grabbing the satchel I entered the parking structure, at this hour it was well shadowed from the bright Arizona sun.

Surreptitiously I glanced northward, the direction from which I had just come. I could see through the ornate rod-iron design that seemed to be haphazardly placed in the wall. My view was all the way to the front doors of the bank.

People were gathering, pointing at the garage...

"The bank just got robbed"

I heard footsteps and in a flash a guy ran past me.

Thank you... Bright Teal Tank-top.

Reaching my car, heartbeat now audible, I opened the unlocked door and tossed the satchel on the floor behind my seat, I started the Lincoln and proceeded to back out of my space.

I needed to suppress the inclination to floor it, burning a hearty patch in the cement would be a telltale signal to anyone with Hero on their mind.

Upon arriving at the gate the gal in the booth quickly said…

"No charge", the red and white stripped arm already in motion.

As I passed the booth I heard her say…

"I think that bank just got robbed"

Trying not to look directly at her…

"Really?"

I reached Camelback Road, which had three eastbound lanes and three to the west, with a center turn lane. Wanting to turn east, I looked only to my left. What luck! No traffic. As I completed my turn and looked to the right I was greeted by three police cars running abreast and they were coming straight at me.

The lights were flashing… no sirens.

I almost did the "Two-Handed Eyeball Cover-up" as they zipped around me. I could hear tires squealing behind me, most likely in front of the bank.

How I didn't hit one of the police cars is a goddamn miracle.

Continuing down Camelback, now heading towards Tempe, my mind was a flurry of thoughts… Stop at the ASU campus, mix in the crowd.
No… it's too close.

Stop… Go… Do SOMETHING.

I found myself headed west, towards the freeway that linked Phoenix with Tucson. Arriving at the on-ramp, I put my blinker on and soon found myself merging with the southbound traffic. I set my cruise control on 59. Home, sixty minutes away.

Please Dear Lord, watch over this idiot. Please… besides, someone needs to feed the dogs.

My brain was on hyper turbo.

I sure hope I'm not going too slow, too cautious is not good.

I left it on 59.

As my garage door rose I was pleased to find that it wasn't filled with police, FBI, guns… all pointed at me as I had imagined. I entered and turned off the engine. The door lowered and then closed. I leaned my head back on the headrest and reached back to touch the canvas bag.

It was there. I closed my eyes and just sat there… a very long time.

I just fulfilled my lifetime fantasy and robbed a freak´n bank!

From my earliest memory I have been fascinated by Bank Robbery. Why I have had this overwhelming desire, how it became so deeply ingrained into my soul or where the actual point of conception took place, I will never know. It has haunted me for more than forty years. I have spent hundreds of hours, from my very early youth to this very day, conceptualizing and devising a method hoping that maybe someday the setting that I have deemed perfect will in fact present itself so that I may fulfill this desire in lieu of being satisfied through vicarious methods.

Today it presented itself.

I grabbed the bag, went into the bedroom and emptied the contents on the bed. Damn, that son-of-a-bitch shorted me. ALOT.

No big deal …. I DID IT!!!

I duct taped the bag & money under a bathroom sink. To say that my weekend was uneventful may be correct, however, there was a lot of window vigilance and a lot of chastising myself… along with disbelief.

Oh yah… and did a little yard work, backyard work.

I didn't sleep at all until Sunday night. What a dose of adrenaline that was.

Monday morning was back to work and I welcomed it like never before. Let's just get everything back to normal, beginning with me not being startled when I hear an ant fart.

A few months passed and I started thinking about what I did and I'm getting a strong urge to do it again .

You did it once, don't press your luck… moron.

Around noon, on a very hot summer day, the starched & pressed Contractor found himself in the Lincoln… northbound. Driving completely through Phoenix I noticed that the exits were becoming less frequent and then a sign… Flagstaff 48 mi.

I got off on the last exit, just prior to the long northward journey. To my surprise it was a major east/west four laner with Shopping malls, a couple of banks and some new Spanish tiled office suites.

Then I saw it… The Scenario.

I parked in just about the same location in the structure as I had at the first bank. I shut off the engine and closed my eyes.

Scotty my man… are you sure?

I opened the glove compartment and grabbed my gun. Why I thought this was necessary, I'll never know. I hadn't taken a gun with me the first time, I had no intention of shooting anyone… no matter what happened.

Maybe myself.

I guess I decided that the gun was required in order to confirm myself a bonafide "Bank Robber"

I walked in the front door looking down at the floor, then glanced up to locate the Managers office.

Same basic floor plan.

As I headed towards the office I noticed a man at the end of cahiers row, leaning on the counter, talking with a young lady.

His casual demeanor caught my attention….. No paperwork!!

A COP!!

You're getting paranoid Scotty, settle down.

Tapping on the door, I waited.

It's not too late to abort...LEAVE NOW!! That guy was a cop.

A young lady opened the door and asked if she could help me. I could see the manager seated behind his desk as I explained the need for clarification; I promised it would only take a moment.
I must have passed the Initial impression once-over because the manager invited me in, already rising with that Banker smile, which comes from smelling the possibility of a LARGE loan. The assistant attempted to excuse herself but I asked if she would please stay and maybe help with the clarification.

She agreed.

Grabbing the note with my fingernails I made the same grand loop, again landing flush.

After making my demands and asking the assistant if she wouldn't mind remaining with me until we were through, I sent the manager off to the vault.

The manager had just cleared the threshold and within a nano-second the assistant began visibly shaking. I mean BOUNCING in her chair.

"Oh no"... "No"... "NO"... "You can't do that!"

This office had a window to the lobby and her reaction was a definite attention alert kind of bounce. I grabbed the note off the desk, with my fingernails of course, and handed it to her...

"Here, pretend you are reading this"

She grabbed the paper with her right hand, which was shaking so fiercely she couldn't grab the other edge of the paper with her left.

It seemed likely you could hear the rattle of the paper all the way to Tucson. Trying to pretend that she was reading proved only to look like she was waving this paper around to solicit attention.

BAD IDEA.

I snapped the paper out of her hand...

"Oh man, I am so sorry, please stop shaking, I am really sorry to put you through this"

Time to bring her out of this almost trans like state...

"Hey there. HEY... HEEEY, WHOA... What is your name?"
"mmMary"

She seemed to have calmed down a bit...

"Do you have children?"
"Yeeees"
"Listen, I am sorry for doing this to you, nobody is going to hurt you, would you like some water... maybe a shot of tequila?"

She looked at me with that... "Say what?" look on her face.

"Well young lady, I sure could use one right now"

She stopped bouncing... A little levity in extremely tense situations never fails to quell a chunk of anxiety.

"This will be over soon and you will be having a Bar-B-Q with your kids this weekend, I promise.... OK?"
"Oookkkay"

On that and just as with the first time, the manager returned, set the bag on the desk and stepped aside. I grabbed the bag, put it in the satchel and headed for the door...

"Thank you very much and Mary…….. Sorry"

When I entered the lobby it was eerily quiet.

Something wasn't right.

With no other option I continued to the door and just as I stepped outside, a head… a head with a helmet peaked around the rough stone entrance wall…

"Hurry up!!! Hurry up!!! The banks getting robbed"
"No shit… REALLY?"

I thought… MAAAN, I'm going to get away with this.

Within half of a step I heard a deafening roar of clicks and looked up to see more cops with guns than I have ever seen gathered in one place and they were ALL pointed at me. A split second later I was hit by what felt like a locomotive and crashed to the ground.

It must have taken numerous seconds before the cobwebs cleared and a few more for the bells to stop ringing, but once they had… I was staring directly into the face of Mr. Casual Demeanor. There were four or five cops hunkered down around me, pinning me to the ground…

"Where are your partners, where are your Mexican partners?"
"I don't have any, I am by myself"
"Bullshit"

He pushed my face into the searing walkway and yelled so all could hear within a one mile radius….

"Look around"
"Hey look, over there….. there they are"

I turned my head and saw that across the street, in front of the mall, were two Mexican looking fellows sitting on a bus stop bench.

A swarm of badges descended upon them and soon they were in the same position as I.

Sure hope those poor bastards aren't illegal's.

With helicopters circling overhead, one with a television camera, I was turned over and frisked.

OH SHIT!! THE FUCKING GUN… IDIOT.

This discovery created quite a stir and after what seemed to be an eternity, being fried on the summer cement in Phoenix, I was picked up and placed into the backseat of a black, unmarked FBI car. The engine was turned off and without the air conditioning it was beyond toasty.

I'm not sure what caused the majority of my later discovered weight loss… Stress, sizzling cement or that hot ass back seat.

After a few hours of witness finger pointing identification and countless high-fives outside the car window, I heard the car start and could only think of one thing…..COME ON AIR CONDITIONING.

The passenger cop seemed to want to talk…

"We've been watching you guys case this bank for quite a while, it was just a matter of time before we got you"
"Truly, I am a solo act, I just drove up here from Tucson and happened to pick this bank randomly"
"If that is true, you are the most unlucky prick in the world, out of over two thousand banking institutions in the Greater Phoenix Valley you picked this one, it's the only one that had a Sting set up… that's like hitting the lottery"

"Yah right, just like hitting the lottery"

I'm not supposed to say anything until I have an Attorney present so our conversation ended there.

Hawaii Five-0 101.

A couple of very excited "Rookie" looking cops opened a side street entrance to the rear of the Police station. I was then placed in a room, handcuffed to the chair leg and for the next eight or so hours had a parade of Interrogators coming in and telling me things would go a lot better for me if I would start talking.

They even did the Good guy/Bad guy thing that I found rather entertaining.

"Sorry, I really want to wait for an Attorney"

Around two in the morning they took me into a holding cell where I remained until they came in with breakfast. A bologna sandwich, small carton of milk and an orange is pretty difficult to choke down, no matter how hungry you are.

I asked for a phone call and about an hour later they opened the cell door and told me I had a five minute phone call coming and I better use it wisely.

Only one chance.

Annie and I had been living together for about six months and I was reasonably sure she would be at the house.

Probably really pissed off that I didn't come home last night and for the first time in my life I had a REAL good excuse.

She answered on the first ring and upon recognizing my voice…

"This better be your "Spirit" I'm talking to, because that's the only excuse I'm going to except"

A 5' 2" looker, she weighed in at around 90 lbs, if you put her on a scale immediately after she jumped into a swimming pool fully clothed…. in a ski outfit complete with parka.

Annie was the first girl that got that "Janie" feeling stirred up again. It felt fucking awesome. I wasn't sure if my rustically glued back together heart would ever function again.

My visitation with the girls kept me updated on Janie's life, so I knew that she had remarried a few years back and was very happy.

Surprisingly, that made me happy.

She deserved it.

From what I could determine the new hubby was a pretty good guy, he filled in as a great Dad and never trash talked me.

The girls always had good things to say about him. They liked him, so I did also.

I was just starting to fall hard and look at what the hell I go out and do. The courting experience for Annie and I looks as though it may take on a new and not so improved look.

Annie was quite different than Janie.

Polar opposites come to mind.

She didn't have a timid bone in her body. Her tiny stature was well supplemented by the lion's heart that ticked inside.

She had ovaries... big ones.

Her kick ass first, take names later attitude was in no way evident when you first lay eyes on her... she was all woman and stood pretty freak'n tall when you got to the Hot & Sexy category.

I felt fortunate to be one of the very few that knew she was really a softie. She didn't like anyone to discover the chink in her armor. It had taken me awhile to convince her that it was a good thing.

She still told me that she would hunt me down and kick my ass good, if I ever told anyone...

"No matter where you may try to hide on this planet, I'll find you"

She even threw in the "Universe" just to make her point well received.

Listen, before we get back to the story... I guess I just let the Cat out of the bag, so if any of you are ever in Tucson and run into a 5' 2" fiery little spinner named Annie, don't say that you read this book or that you know where I am.

This is an advisory for your safety, as well as mine

Enough said.

... "Annie, please listen to me because I've got a BIG problem"

"Ok, but you had better have a real good excuse"

"Right now I'm in jail and they only gave me this one five minute call"

"IN JAIL!!! Scott Andrew, this better not be a joke.... What for?"

"Bank Robbery"

"Well did you tell them that they have the wrong person?"

"That's my BIG problem cutie ... they don't"

There was a loud click, then silence...

"Your five minutes are up sir"

On the way back to the cell I asked the guard if he knew when I would get another phone call...

"Tomorrow morning"

After the longest 24 hours I have ever spent, my cell door opened and I was led back to the phone...

"Annie, please just listen to me... First, have the cops been to the house?"

"No"

"Well, expect them... you need to get your stuff and get out, the Lincoln is in a parking garage on Bell Road and I-17, the keys are on the driver side floor. Please go get it ... you can have it"

"Scott Andrew Frieze... what did you do?"

"Annie, aaah Annie.... DAAAAAMN. I'm in the Phoenix main jail, try to see if you can visit with me and please just get out of the house, I don't want you involved"

CLICK...

"Your five minutes are up sir"

Early Monday morning I was summoned from my cell and told that I had an Arraignment hearing.

"I need an Attorney"
"There has been one appointed to you"

Upon entering the courtroom I noticed a disheveled looking character sitting at the desk and thought...

"Oh, no"

Yep, that was my Attorney and just when I thought things couldn't get worse...

"Ah... you must be William Johnson, please take a seat"

William??? WTF... This isn't going to be good

Pre-Trial

A slam-dunk arraignment by the Prosecution had me on a bus to CCA Florence, Arizona. An in the middle of the desert long term, pre-trial holding facility.

A different civilization… with different rules.

The following Friday morning I was summoned to the Tower, a well fortified plexi-glass and steel bar fortress within the fortress that kept the guards separated from us. The tower was placed where every nook, cranny and sphincter could be viewed without their having to exert themselves.

"Mr. Frieze, you have a visitor… get ready"

I cleaned up the best I could, clean clothes were scarce if you haven't figured out the barter system… I hadn't. After stripping and being thoroughly searched I was led into a room with two very long benches divided by a wire enforced glass barrier. About every twenty four inches or so, hung a phone. My seat was pointed out to me and after a few minutes the door opened on the other side of the barrier. A parade of mostly women entered the room and then there she was… beautiful Annie.

After about thirty minutes of my how & why, I received a promise from her to contact my family and to return the next visitation day.

With a unanimous decision on my being "the biggest Idiot on the face of this earth EVER, since the creation of mankind", we pushed our hands together, the plexi-glass unable to deny me the feel her warmth.

Daaaamn.... I really screwed up.

After a few days of chastising myself with a constant barrage of, "How in the hell did I get so stupid as to screw up my life like this" running through my mind, I was again summoned to the tower and informed of a pending visit.

This time I had clean clothes to put on.

Same room, however this time it was my older brother, Tim.

He also insisted on my personal confirmation on being an absolute moron. Man... if this keeps up I'm going to have quite a complex to deal with once this is over with, IF there is such a thing as an over with.

... "Tim, I need you to find me an Attorney... a good one, I could be in here for the rest of my life. Please bro... I truly need you to help me"

After another l-o-o-o-n-g two weeks the men in the tower requested my presence once more, however, this time I was told I had an Attorney visit.

Wonderful, Mr. Disheveled.

To my un-measurable delight a well-dressed gentleman stepped into the room and asked if I was Scott Andrew Frieze.

Good start, the right name right out of the gate.

Thanks Tim.

He looked to be a no-nonsense kind of guy.

"My name is Marcus Guerrero, your brother Tim has retained me to represent you as it pertains to your legal matters, is that alright with you?"

I couldn't say yes fast enough.

He started right in…

"Let's review the charges"…
"Two counts of Bank Robbery, mandatory minimum five years each, two counts of Use of a Firearm while committing a Felony, mandatory minimum ten years each, two counts of Holding a Person without their Consent, mandatory minimum twenty years"

He raised his eyes from the document…

"Each"
"EACH???"
"That's the big one Scott, then there is Public Endangerment and probably a few other charges they will think of to throw in. Unfortunately this case has been assigned to a Prosecutor by the name of Christopher Hyman, a real Ass who doesn't like to plea bargain. They are also trying to clear the books on a couple of unsolved robberies, so don't be surprised if they try to chuck those into the pile. Now, your brother has told me a little about you, but why don't you start with telling me a little about yourself and then explain to me what in the heck were you doing"

The first thing out of my mouth…

"Hey… I didn't take a gun with me on that first robbery"

He looked at me with Pity written all over his face…

"Scott… a tiny drop of water in this very large body of water, please… about yourself"

For the next eight months he would pop in, give me a progress report and then leave.

I liked him… felt I was in good hands.

About one year to the date, after my crimes, Marcus stopped in and explained to me the Draw process between the six Federal Judges for assigning upcoming cases.

"Scott… you drew Judge Goldstein, the worst of the lot. He is known for handing out Maximums, he's mean and he absolutely hates criminals. I'm sorry to bring you this news. I believe it's time to have a little sit down with Mr. Hyman"

Reality was that with the simple addition of the Minimums I had well surpassed the average expected mortality of a male human being.

I'm NEVER going to be free again.

About a week later Marcus showed up…

"I think that I can get Mr. Hyman to accept a thirty year plea bargain and I believe you should strongly consider this option. It may be your only chance to see a little bit of freedom. Scott, they caught you in the act… a strong case"

I'll be seventy two years old.

"With Good time credit figured in that would mean you would only have to do a little over twenty six years"

Ah, much better…. I'll be a little over sixty eight...

"Scott, I know this is a lot to heap on your plate right now, but I need to know how you want me to proceed, our day in court has been scheduled… we have five weeks. I'll be back in one week for your answer"

Like clockwork, one week later the Tower beckoned, informing me on the arrival of my Attorney. I had been dressed for hours.

Marcus stepped in and without formalities …

"What is it going to be?"
"I have a couple of questions that I would like to ask you regarding Plea Bargain, Trial by Judge and Trial by Jury"

After confirming what I had already thought to be true, I put my head on the table for a moment…

"I want a Trial by Judge. You, me, Christopher Hyman and Judge Goldstein. I believe it is my only chance to recover a normal life once I am free again"

Marcus looked at me for what seemed to be an eternity…

"Then we have a lot of work to do"

My workload consisted of contacting family, relatives, friends, employers; anyone I felt would either make an appearance on my behalf or write a letter to the court supporting me.

The next month seemed like only days when I found myself on the bus headed for downtown Phoenix. I was shuffled into the courtroom, a Federal Marshal on each side, one to the rear. I had been shackled at the ankles, my wrists were cuffed and secured to a six inch wide leather waist belt with an apparatus they called Black Box which restricts the bearer from moving arms, wrists and hands. It was quite painful.

All ordered by Mr. Christopher Hyman, Federal Prosecutor.

I heard whispering and looked up to see the small courtroom filled with the faces I knew so well… Mom, Dad, Stepdad, my sister Joan, with my brother-in-law Robert, my brother Tim, with his wonderful wife Lynn… my entire family, some of my cousins, past & present friends and of course, Annie. I wanted to look into each face but was abruptly seated and told to look forward and NOT to look into the gallery again.

Being so enthralled with the display of support I hadn't noticed that all representatives were present and seated. Marcus leaned towards me …

"Are you alright?"
"Yah, I think so… but this Black Box is killing me"

Marcus looked over to his right…

"Chris, you think you can have these cuffs removed?"

I heard his voice for the first time…

"Well, can you assure me that your client won't try something stupid"

Sighing loudly Marcus said…

"Chris"

After too long of a pause…

"Ok, but the ankle cuffs stay on"

Marcus muttered…

"Asshole"

"All rise for his Honor Federal Judge Howard D. Goldstein…"

As I started to rise my faithful matching Marshal bookends appeared, I guess to make sure that I wasn't going to try something stupid.

He had a head full of thick platinum, highlighted by crystal clear aqua blue eyes. To complete the package was a perfectly chiseled sneer.

A rather tall fellow.

The Marshals pressing me into the seated position snapped me back to reality. I noticed everyone glaring at me, including Judge Goldstein, from their already seated positions.

The word Awe isn't sufficient.

A deep voice broke the silence...

"Mr. Hyman, Mr. Guerrero, are we ready to proceed?"
"We are your Honor"
"Mr. Frieze, I have read the files and have reviewed the charge's, I also understand that you have chosen this forum and that the only charge you are disputing is Holding a Person without their Consent, is that correct?"

I could hear my mom sniffling.

Marcus patted me on the knee.

"Yes your Honor"
"Mr. Guerrero has informed me that you have agreed to a rather informal hearing, you are open to questions and that you will be forthright when answering.... is that correct?"
"Yes Sir"
"Well then. I have one... when you were apprehended at the bank the reports indicate that there weren't any traces of drugs or alcohol in your system, you were gainfully employed and had been for some time. My review of your W-2 forms seem to indicate that your income was well above the average, what in the HELL prompted you to do what you did?"

Marcus murmured...

"Stay calm...THINK about what you are saying"

This is IT, the rest of my life DEPENDS on what I say......STAY CALM.
It's hard to remember exactly what I did say. I just remember I told the truth, starting with being a little boy that wanted to be a Bank Robber and ended with...

"And that, your Honor, is the very simple and extremely stupid reason I did what I did"

When I sat back down I noticed that Judge Goldstein had his hands clasped in front of him on his desk, he was kind of hunkered down and forward over his hands... it looked like he had the break of a smile at the corner of his mouth.

Marcus whispered...

"Well done"
"Mr. Hyman... with respect to the only disputed charge, I understand you would like to introduce the testimony of one of the victims"
"Yes your Honor... may I call Mary Tomlinson forward"

Uh oh... The bouncing lady, Mary.

I've got SERIOUS problems.

In walked Mary, the gal I had frightened half to death in the Managers office that final day of my life... as I knew it. She looked even smaller than I had remembered, more frail...... vulnerable.

As the bailiff did his swearing in I thought... Scotty my boy, you deserve everything they throw at you for invading this poor women's life.

"Now Ms. Tomlinson.... do you see the person, in this courtroom today, that entered the Managers office on June 13, 1996, with the intention of Robbing your place of employment, namely the Wells Fargo Bank located at ---------- If so, would you please point out this person to the court"

I had been looking down at the table-top in front of me, completely overcome with shame but could feel her eyes on me and the sense of her finger.

... "Please let the court record that the Defendant, Mr. Scott Andrew Frieze has been identified"

Now after Mr. Frieze entered…"

Chris was in his groove now, recounting every detail fairly accurately, but when he said…

"Now after Mr. Frieze told Mr. Wilson, your Manager, to go into the vault, he told you to stay with him until Mr. Wilson returned with the money… is that correct?"
"Yes"

He had my complete attention.

"I have a diagram of the office where you first encountered Mr. Frieze, would you please take a good look at this and tell me if it is accurate… please pay particular attention to the location of the door, window, desk and chairs"

After a minute or so…

"Yes, it is accurate"
"Now, Mr. Frieze was seated in the chair identified with the A
….is that correct?"
"Yes"
"He asked you to be seated in the chair identified with the B
… is that correct?"
"Yes"
"Well, if the diagram of the office is accurate, Mr. Frieze had been seated in chair A and he had you seated in chair B, he was between you and the exit. Is that correct?"
"Yes"
"Then it would be correct to say that he was blocking you from the exit… is that correct?"
"Yes"

Mary had been looking directly at Christopher Hyman throughout this entire Q & A.

Suddenly, without any reason, Mary turned and looked directly at me. I happened to be looking at her at that very moment and our eyes locked.

Just a split second.

An octave louder….

"Now Ms. Tomlinson…"

I could tell that Chris didn't like the fact that he lost her attention…

"So, if you wanted to get up and leave you would not have been able to"

There was a discernible pause, not a sound…

"Well…. Maybe"

You could see Chris's neck turn red and he brightened as the coloration continued, all the way to his hairline…

"Let me re-phrase my question… Mr. Frieze told you to be seated in chair B and you were NOT able to leave because Mr. Frieze, seated in the chair marked A, was blocking you from the exit"
"I don't know…. I didn't try…. he seemed to be worried because I got scared ….he was very nice"

Mr. Christopher Hyman Federal Prosecutor stood there, his mouth hanging open all the way down to the floor, with… I CAN'T BELIEVE SHE JUST SAID THAT, written across his forehead.

… "Your Honor, may I request a break Sir?"
"It is close to 11:45, we will resume at 1 pm, please remove Mr. Frieze until then"

I had been sitting in my tiny holding cell trying to eat my standard issue dry bologna sandwich, carton of milk and orange for about an hour when Marcus arrived...

"God damn Scott... do you know what just happened in there? Christopher Hyman is ONE pissed off dude. I think that episode just removed 40 years off your sentence. Holy Crap... in all my years I've never seen testimony fall apart like that before. I've heard about it happening, but have never witnessed it and thank God it wasn't MY witness. SON OF A BITCH THAT WAS GREAT"

"All rise for the Honorable Federal Judge Howard D. Goldstein"

Marcus whispered....

"Ok Scott, stay calm"

I think I should have been saying this to him. He was as giddy as a school girl that just got asked to her first Prom.

"Mr. Hyman has informed me that the Prosecution has no further witnesses... Mr. Guerrero, I understand that you have testimony on behalf of Mr. Frieze"
"Yes your honor"

For the next hour and a half my family and friends came forward...

"Yes, Scotty has had this desire in his mind since childhood, he is really a caring father... brother... friend..."

My Mom broke down in tears, so did my Dad.... It was tough.

The thunderous voice ruptured the uncomfortable pause that seemed to have manifested.

"Unless the attorneys have further testimony to introduce I would like to take a break here. I believe I will be ready to render a decision and pronounce sentencing before day's end. Are all parties in agreement with this?"
"Mr. Hyman?"
"Yes your Honor"
"Mr. Guerrero?"
"Yes your Honor"
"Mr. Frieze?"
"Yes Sir"

"All rise for the Honorable Federal Judge Howard D. Goldstein"

Marcus put his hand on my forearm...

"Well, this is it. I sure hope we made the right decision"
"This has been a unique case, I have considered all that has been documented, along with the testimony. I have read all the letters sent to this court regarding this case, including an impressive letter of support sent to me by the past Governor of New Mexico and his wife, Anthony and Lupita Avila. Mr. Frieze, would you please rise"

Marcus stood up with me.

... "My decision is as follows; On the two counts of Bank Robbery I find Mr. Frieze.... Guilty. On the two counts of Use of a Firearm during the Commission of a Felony, I have reduced the charge to 1 count and find Mr. Frieze... Guilty. On the 2 counts of Holding a Person without their Consent, this serious matter is what I have had to consider extensively for which, if charged, would end Mr. Frieze ever having hope in being released back into society"

I don't know if Judge Goldstein was pausing for the effect or if he was still deliberating, but I had been holding my breath so long I was feeling wobbly.

"My decision on this is that the Prosecution was unable to prove to me that Ms. Tomlinson was unable to leave that office for reason of restraint by Mr. Frieze. Because there wasn't any further testimony in regards to the second count of Holding a Person without their Consent, I have no choice but to find Mr. Frieze ….. Not Guilty"

I think the only reason I started breathing again had been to get the circulation of my blood back into the arm Marcus had restricted the blood flow to with his meant to be comforting death grip.

All I heard Marcus say was "Holy Shit" and could hear various forms of Yahoo from behind me but distinctly remember my sister say… "Oooh Scotty, we love you"

Christopher Hyman was not hiding his annoyance, but looked to be keeping busy arraigning and stacking his files.

The bailiff bellowed…

"Quiet Please"
"All parties have agreed to allow sentencing immediately after my findings, is that correct Mr. Hyman?"

Chris was busy pouting, but Judge Goldstein wasn't having any of that….

"MISTER HYMAN?"

After reaching what Chris probably knew was the limit of the pause…

"Yes…...............… Your Honor"

Judge Goldstein glared at him a few more seconds…

"Mr. Guerrero?"
"Yes your Honor"
"Mr. Frieze?"
"Yes your Honor"
"Will Mr. Frieze please rise once more"

Judge Goldstein started handing down the sentence but frankly lost me with using the terminology "To be carried out Consecutively" and "To be carried out Concurrently".

When he had finally finished with all the legalize….

"96 months, with credit for time served. Mr. Frieze, I had better not EVER see you in this courtroom again and suggest should you have any more of these Childhood Fantasies that they remain as such"

The gavel cracked, breaking the silence in the room.

Chris Hyman picked up his files and slammed them down on the table in front of him.

"MISTER HYMAN … I will NOT tolerate that type of display in MY courtroom, if you don't agree with the findings I believe you know the remedies afforded you… throwing your files down is NOT one of them"

CRAAACK…..

"CASE CLOSED"

My Bookends were busy cuffing me. Marcus was busy shaking my brothers' hands and hugging my Mom and sister... my sister twice.

I was busy trying not to pass out on the floor. Holy Jesus, I'm going to be free again. As I was being led through the back door I heard my sister yell out... "You made it, hang in there... we love you"

It had to be close to 5pm by the time I stepped into the "Hold for Transport" cell where I was greeted by eleven of my fellow Inmates, the majority of them didn't fare so well.

I had difficulties keeping my elation in check.

The transport team arrived and called out nine names, mine was not one of them.

Around midnight I heard chains rattling, the cell door opened and I was told to step out.

The bus must have made stops along the way because there were a lot less Orange jumpsuits on it than when we began. I had slept so deeply that completely waking up was difficult.

When I glanced out the window I woke up fast.

The bus was rolling across what looked to be a five lane highway, each lane divided from the others by very tall razor wire fences.

As we passed under what I thought was a bridge I looked up to discover that it was a tower, complete with shotgun toting sentries.

Prison

The check-in procedure was basically the same as CCA. You leave everything you had on you in the Admission cell, then step through to the de-lousing showers. Once they deem you adequately sprayed, you step into your new world in the same manner you came into the old... with only what God provided.

I spent the first 48 hours in an Isolation cell, what they call Suicide Watch. They want to make sure you are mentally ready for your new home. Not that I had any intentions, but being placed in a concrete room, dressed only in boxers, how in the hell could you do yourself in? No shoe laces, no belt... I guess you could bang your head on the floor, but then you would just knock yourself out before you croaked... wouldn't you?

Anyway... with no books, TV, radio or human contact, that's what I thought about my first two days in The Big House.

When the door finally opened and I was led into a room with a caged counter. I was given 2 boxers, 2 t-shirts, 2 pants, 2 shirts, 2 socks, a pair of steel-toed boots and a belt.

A BELT!! Why didn't they give that to me 48 hrs ago

After a couple more hours in a holding cell getting to know two other Fish we were handed our towel, soap, toothbrush and 1 roll of toilet paper.

A particularly LARGE guard appeared from nowhere…

"Don't lose your TP, you only get 1 roll a week, now follow me and DO NOT stray off the yellow painted line on the floor"

Between maneuvering various corridors with buzz in barriers at each end and keeping your eye on the yellow line, a return trip to freedom for the unfamiliar was doubtful.

Well designed boys.

As our march continued I noticed the barriers were becoming more fortified, more menacing. We came upon the Cat Daddy of all… Bars w/guards, walk 15´… double bars w/guards, 25´ further… double steel doors w/guards & metal detector.

Coming from two and a half days inside a building, then stepping into the Arizona sunshine everyone's armload of personal belongings were quickly raised overhead trying to shield blinded eyes. As my vision slowly returned the first thing I noticed was a lack of greenery. Horizon to horizon all you could see was sand and rock with an occasional cactus. All viewed through multiple rows of razor-wire. This did not have the manicured grass, flower beds and potted palms that I noticed when I entered the Admissions and Visitation buildings up front. This was steel & concrete, dirt and rocks void of vegetation and rows upon rows of razor wire framing every border that was up, down or to the side.

A shit load of razor wire complete with the customary, Caution High Voltage signs every 15 feet.

From what I had learned from talking with guys coming through CCA Florence that were on their way to court, most Prison Systems are similar.

One similarity is "Movement"

An on the hour siren that alerts all that you have 10 minutes to move to your next desired location. You had better get to where you need to be because if you don't make it by the next alert you are "Out of Bounds" a our next UN-desired move will be just as the song goes, "Thirty days in the Hole".

We were led to where I could see 3-four level hexagon shaped buildings.

The guards stopped at a small one level housing unit with Low Level Custody in front. It was detached from everything else and behind the medical building, something you couldn't see until you were there. I was kept on the walkway by two guards and the other two escorted my companions to the door.

The two returned and we continued on down the walkway.

We passed a dirt soccer field and a small building that had REC stenciled above the door, finally stopping at a three way fork. My escorts seemed to be puzzled about which path to take so we halted. A radio was pulled from an overloaded waist rack while the others consulted the clipboard.

This gave me a chance to take in my new neighborhood.

The buildings were not hexagonal as I had thought, they were more like the shape of a Stealth bomber, the cockpit being the entrance.

Only the building on the right had a fence that completely surrounded it, isolation from all else.

"Let's move Frieze"

We all started down the path to the right.

Upon arrival at the iron fortified six inch thick barrier, apparently the designers idea for a front door, my personal possessions were thoroughly searched with even greater vigilance than when searched at the gate in the razor wire laden fence that insured the buildings seclusion from all else.

Housing Unit A.

Once inside I found myself in a kind of anti-chamber where we were greeted by another two guards and I was summarily transferred over to their care. They took me to the right wing where immediately upon entering there was a large room with about twenty bunk beds...

"Try to find yourself a bed or just pull up some floor. We don't have any lockers so I suggest you keep all your shit with you. If you lose it... to bad, it won't get replaced until next week. One of the Counselors will call you in and explain the rules"

He turned and walked away. I stood there for a moment taking in my new digs with my 40 new roommates.

The Piranha feed was on... new fish in the pond.

"Hey dude, I got a place for you over here. It's nice, close to the bathrooms and everything."
"No thanks bro, I'll find a spot"
"Yo Holmes, you just get'n in, bunch of us got a spot over there"

He pointed over to a corner that had four or five guys in it and they were all giving me the head to toe.

"Appreciate it man... I just want to take in the sights for a minute, I might take you up on the offer"
"You know skin takes care of its own"
"Yah brother, I do"
"I'm Sling, you need something Sling'l handle it for you"

He stood there with me as I looked around; I quickly determined that Sling's offer was going to be my best option.

"Sling, let's go on over and check out your house... you can introduce me to the other Peckerwoods"

Different civilization, different rules, different language.

They all had Sling kind of monikers, but were basically all right dudes, all in their early twenties, that got caught selling drugs. If they were here it meant that they were moving or trying to move a lot, especially if they were in this building.

Through conversation with the Moniker boys I had discovered that this building was the Max.

That goddamn gun that I wasn't going to use proved to be very costly. A firearm in a Federal building is severely frowned upon. A bank is considered a Federal building because it is FDIC.

Bottom line: Idiot for robbing a bank. Super Moron for taking a gun with me.

I was offered a 2´x 6´ spot on the floor against the wall. It looked as good as I could hope to find so I settled in for the night. They wanted me to go with them to the Chow Hall and I needed a little contemplation time regarding my future. Just 24 hours ago I was on my way to court. I am now laying on the floor in a Maximum Security Housing Unit at a Federal Prison.

Overwhelming.

"You sure you don't want to go get chow?"
"Nah... thanks, I'll just stay here and hold down the fort"
"Huh?"
"No thanks bro, I'm not hungry"

The fish bowl, which was the aptly named room that I was now calling home, became a very popular place to stroll by for every Shark, Predator and Fag after the Chow Hall closed.

The wall that joined it with the main housing area was wire enforced glass. A perfect place to window shop the new fish... a fish being anyone new to the prison.

The counselor called me in the next morning and basically told me that I was on my own...

"If you need something, figure it out, if you can't and you screw things up, you go to the Hole. Is there anything else I can help you with Mr. Frieze?"
"No, but thank you very much, you have been quite helpful"

Figuring out who are the Hustlers and the Predators is your first task at hand. Once determined, you find out where they are assigned and what shift they are working. Then you have to go through the same process all over again, this time with your fellow convicts.

There was only one way to get out of the fish bowl. You had to find someone that was about to get released, then go talk to the guy he shared the cell with and if you are compatible, you got yourself a Celly and you move in to your permanent house.

You just have to hope that the guy that's short doesn't do anything stupid and get more time tacked on before he's released.

Smoking was a nerve calmer for me so at every movement I would go to the smoking area and puff away for nine minutes.

That's where I met Alfredo.

Normal looking vato, from LA where I grew up, he was in for drugs. He told me that he was looking for a Celly because his was leaving in ten days.

I'm a pretty clean guy and the only thing that concerned me about Alfredo was that he was kind of scruffy look'n and unshaven, which led me to believe he might be a pig. I did a couple of drive-bys and his cell looked to be kept clean, so I figured I lucked out and found a Celly quick. I'm pretty much a keep to myself kind of guy so I carried on with figuring out the Routine and didn't talk much with anyone.

On Sunday mornings you get an hour in the yard so I went out early to the smoking area hoping to see Alfredo, I hadn't seen him for a few days and I wanted to make sure everything was cool with moving in. I heard a couple guys say… "Uh oh... here comes the Sunday Princess" so I turned to look to where they were pointing. Down the walkway, coming towards us was Alfredo or should I say Alfreda. His hair was gelled straight up in an Edward Scissor hands doo, hot-pants modified from gym shorts and a visitation shirt tied up under his boobs to look like one of the Dukes of Hazard chicks…. Boobs?
HOLY SHIT, he's got boobs.

… "CELLI… YOO HOO!!! CELLI… Hiiii… there you are Scotty"
"Hey… Alfredo, quit fucking screaming… WHAT THE FUCK DUDE, this isn't funny. WHAT IN THE FUCK ARE YOU DOING?"
"Whaaat? If you mean my make-up, whaaaat??? you don't like it??? I make it from kool-aid that I steal from the kitchen. What's the matter Scotty?"
"Are you FUCKING kidding… What's the matter? I'm not into this kind of shit, THAT'S the God damn matter"
"Don't you think you should of mentioned to me that you like to dress like a chick?"
"I wanted to pick out material with you today… from a book my mother sent me, she was going to make curtains for our cell"

He started to cry.

"Whoooa ... Alfredo... Whooa... STOP THAT CRYING SHIT... come on man, don't do this to me. Look bro, I'm just trying to make it another six and half years by flying under the radar, being your Celly would be like flying right into the Dish. You're probably an alright dude, a little kinked out in my book, but hey to each his own"
"Does this mean you're not mov..."
"God damn Alfredo... NO"

Six days in the fish bowl and counting.

The Moniker boys are OK, but it's time to move on and try to get a permanent cell so I can start working on what I want to accomplish during this pause in my life.

Another week went by until a lucky encounter, while waiting in line for my 1 day a week commissary visit, gave me some promise. The guy in front of me mentioned that his Celly was going to be leaving in two weeks. They had been sharing a cell for twenty three years. After confirming that he wasn't a Kink, I mentioned that I was looking for a permanent spot.

We planned on meeting at chow the following morning to discuss it.

Frank had been a "Cooker" in Montana and received a thirty five year sentence for excelling in his craft. After Good Time was factored in he only had six to go. The fact that I had a little over six left to do meant that Frank didn't need to go through the Celly selection process again. He liked that and I liked the fact that he had things figured out pretty good with twenty plus down. It was a huge stress reliever to get behind closed doors.

Spending the better part of a month on the floor in the fish bowl served as one hell of a window into the life and times of a criminal. Forty of them… twenty four seven. Well, I guess there was forty one of us, if you want to count me.

As crazy as this is going to sound, I don't consider myself a criminal.

A criminal harms people, property, the normal flow of society… in my mind a criminal basically affects, infects, interrupts or damages society in such a way that his further participation would precipitate the continuance of the decline/decay.

Just answer one question… Does Bank Robbery fit into one of those categories?

Interrupts the normal flow of society? Maybe. Well, yes… it interrupted a couple of people's normal routine and caused undue anxiety. I knew what I was doing was against the law and should I be caught I would have to spend time in jail as a punishment. Accepting that, I went out and fulfilled a childhood dream. I was caught in the act. Although I did not receive the fifty plus year sentence Christopher Hyman sorely wanted me to receive, the 96 months I was handed is not just a slap on the wrist.

If you think so, Why don't you drop on by and spend the night with us, I'll leave the cell light on for ya.

Thank God that I drew Howard D. Goldstein… an astute and fair gentleman, a wise judge of man.

It has literally been months since I have been able to sleep through the night. I awoke the first morning in my house feeling well rested, clearheaded and ready to get going on my… Scotty's Self Improvement in just 6 years plan.

I enjoyed a wonderful breakfast consisting of watery powdered eggs, two strips of bacon that had never experienced a heated surface, an orange and a carton of milk that someone must have stolen from a kindergarten lunch pail.

I returned to Unit A and headed for the house to fine tune my plan. Three steps from the door I heard my name being called on the PA system… "Inmate Frieze, report to Unit A Command Center"

Trying not to flop around like the fish out of water that I was, I headed directly towards the location where there always seemed to be guards.

BAM!! The Command Center.

I had been greeted by a sniveley looking youngster sitting in a fortified iron box reception booth, he looked like he was wearing his overweight grandpa's security guard uniform…

"Inmate Frieze, you are to report to Lt. Smiley over at the chow hall on the next movement… twenty five minutes"

Upon arriving I realized that I didn't have a clue who this Lt. Smiley was and having already noticed that guys that ask fish questions draw unnecessary attention to themselves I decided to just look around and try to spot a guy that had a big ass grin on his face.

A guard with a little more color and brass on his uniform than most, walked up to me… minus a smile.

"Inmate Frieze?"
"Yes"
"Go on back to the warehouse and report to Inmate Gutierrez… you will be assigned to work there from 7 am to 5 pm Monday thru Friday"

"Work? Sir, I did not have plans to work while I'm in here. I heard that there is some educational material in the Prison library"
"Well I planned that you work. You will be paid and you can use this money to buy commissary each week. Now go report to Gutierrez"

After a little reconsideration on my part I decided a day's work might be good for a little exercise and I could use a little money until I can get the materials I want for the SSIIJ6Y plan.

I entered a huge warehouse that was clearly the distribution hub of all the products used in the running of a prison. Immediately one of the convicts walked up to me and asked if I was Frieze. I didn't need to ask him if he was Gutierrez, it was stenciled on his shirt... along with his numbers.

My monogrammed prison issue wouldn't be ready for another couple of days. That's the day you lose the fins & scales and all the crap that goes along with it.

"Yah... I'm Frieze"
"Follow me... I'll show you around"

Rudy Gutierrez turned out to be an alright dude. He was just trying to get through what was left of his life, which will be accomplished right here in this very warehouse.

He was serving two life terms for burning down his business.

"Two life terms for burning down your business, fuck dude, who was your Attorney?"
"Man.., I had a great Attorney, he saved me from the needle and got me this Federal gig instead of State... it's a little easier here"
"Still bro... Life??... for burning down a business?"
"My partners were in it"

WHOOOOA... GOOOOOOD MORN'N.

"Sooo... Lt. Smiley told me that we get paid for working here... what is it?... like, minimum wage or something?"

The way he was taking everything in stride, it looked to me that he was still pleased with his decision to bring a five gallon can of gas and a Bic to work with him that day.

."Well Scott... it was Scott, right... well Scott, it's not quite minimum wage"

As we were walking I thought I saw something move up in the rafters, they had to be at least thirty feet off the ground. Some of them were twenty feet tall and the rafters were ten above those.

There were double deck ramps for the fork-lifts.

We finished with the tour and started walking back towards the entrance.

"There aren't any deliveries today and we're caught up with most of the stocking so I guess I'll just see you tomorrow. Whatever you do, do not go out those doors until you hear the siren, then go directly to your house"
"By the way... what is the pay scale here?"

He looked at me in surprise, chuckled...

"Well... you really don't know, do you?"

Just then the phone started ringing... he threw up the one finger gimme a moment sign and ran off.

There was that movement in the rafters again. I tried to focus in on the heights above the dome warehouse lamps that were hanging from the support beams.

There it was again.

As my eyes adjusted I could finally make out the silhouette. There was a little Mexican guy hanging from one of the beams by one leg and one arm. He was trying to reach for something in a box on the very top of one of the racks. I watched as he let go with the other arm so he could open the box. He was hanging thirty plus feet above the ground by only one leg. He removed what looked to be one of those big #10 cans of something meant for commercial kitchens, raised the can up towards the rafters and out of the darkness came a hand that relieved hanging dude of his burden.

As my eyes became more adapted to the darkness I could make out several guys up there forming a human delivery chain.

Someone up there, probably the spotter, must have said something to hanging dude because he looked directly at me, he had a big smile on his face, I could see his teeth glowing through the darkness.

He raised a finger to his lips as to make sure I don't say anything and went back into the box to snag anther can.

That was freaking amazing.

I got a huge smile, almost laughing out loud.

"Hey Scott, what are you smiling about?"
"Oh, hey Rudy… I didn't see you roll up"
"Tell me what's got you smiling so big, I could use hearing something funny after THAT phone call"
"Ah… I'm just so fucking happy to be here Rudy… that's all"

He looked at me kind of puzzled, then shook it off and then said…

"Twelve cents a day"
"What's twelve cents a day?"

The siren rattled my bones and just about blasted my ear drums out. I need to find that goddamn volume knob if I'm going to work in here.

"You better get going Scott... you don't want to catch that second siren on the outside"

I started to take off, then turned back to Rudy..

"What's twelve cents a day?"

I couldn't hear his words because of the siren blast, but I sure could read his lips... YOUR PAY.

He must have meant an hour... twelve cents a day? That's impossible, there is no way someone would only pay a human being twelve cents a day for labor in this day & age.

Not in America, I even think that's against the law, isn't it?

I carried on with this debate in my mind until I saw Frank that evening...

"The guy in the warehouse said that the pay for working there is twelve cents... A DAY. That can't be right, could it? He must have meant an hour... didn't he?"
"That's one of the better paying jobs... kitchen get eight cents"
"A DAY?"
"Yes siree. You notice that the kitchen is staffed with all the illegal's? Those boys are in hog heaven. Never had it better in Mexico or on the street. Room, electricity, cable tv, hot showers. Working in the kitchen they can eat anything they want. All the cheese, ground beef, chicken, eggs and tortillas they can get away with is sold to the others in Unit B. On Saturdays you can get some of the best Mexican food in Arizona... best one stamp burrito on earth."

"You're a clerk… you mind me asking what you make?"

"Well, I probably wouldn't do it all over again, but I've been doing it for so long, about twenty two years, I'm pretty settled in. They pay me twenty seven cents a day. I've never touched it. I'm just letting it pile up. It won't be a big pile, I just don't want them to think I'm accepting that as my worth, you know what I mean. They won't know if I withdraw it or not when I get out. Maybe I'll never touch it, make em account for it at every years end until dooms day"

"I like that Frank… I hope you leave it in. Now, I'm having a bit of a problem justifying my working while I'm in here…. What's the deal, do they make you work?"

"Did you go to school… did you graduate High School?"

"Yah… of course"

"In here, there is no "of course" to that question. As you'll find out, most of the guys in here didn't get past the sixth grade. That reminds me, if someone wants you to read something funny in a letter that a family member sent them, it'll go a long way if you read the whole letter out loud, so they can hear ya. Don't clown em if there isn't anything funny and don't comment about the content. Just hand it back to 'em. I look at it as part of the deal for being fortunate enough to have had the opportunity to be educated."

"Damn Frank… there IS some compassion within these walls, you just picked up my spirits"

I didn't feel like going to the chow hall once again. Maybe it was the manner in which they made the announcement. Each of the six wings that housed approximately one hundred seventy five convicts got called in rotation.

Each week the rotation changed depending on the weekly cleanliness report. I was alright with all of that, it didn't matter to me whether I ate at five, in between, or the six thirty last call.

What bothered me was the screaming of "CHOOOW"… "CHOOOW" …. "CHOOOW" over the units PA system.

Always three freakin times.

It made me feel like a cow being called in to the cattle trough from the barren range. Frank and two others were always let out first, no matter what the rotation order was.

I think it was Clerks Privileges.

I had the top bunk and as I lay there reading one of the books I grabbed off the book cart and felt a presence.
It's not hard to notice any change in or around a six foot by ten foot cell. I glanced at the opening where the door had been retracted for the call to CHOOOW.

About twelve inches just inside the door stood two black dudes. Just outside the door, doing the left-right-left-right spotter job, stood another. They weren't six footers... but they were each about as thick as a '55 Buick Road Master. Obviously card carrying members of the Weight Pile.

We all just looked at each other, no-one said anything, then as fast as they appeared... they disappeared.

It wasn't fifteen seconds later when a set of keys came strolling by.
I was sure that these were the same guys that never missed an evening of window shopping at the fish bowl during my stay there.

I decided to work at the warehouse for the time being, a way to learn about the neighborhood. When I wasn't working I kept my eye out for those three characters. One thing for sure, they weren't housed in the right wing.

This building was well secured, entrances and exits, which meant they lived in the left wing.

I had been well schooled on what would be the standard entrance exam administered to a fish, once settled in with the general population. I even had the unfortunate experience of viewing first hand examples of the repercussions if you received a failing grade. I had been told that no one was exempt.

It was just that I had hoped it would be delayed a bit longer.

The only way to answer a Predators inquisitional encounter was with an absolutely fearless and unequivocally powerful response that wouldn't be forgotten. Any response short of that would have every Shark, Predator and Dominant personality within this compound smelling the blood and promptly joining in on the feed.

These Type-A pricks are looking for the weak or injured so they can nibble on the carcass at their leisure. The last thing they want is prey that is willing to go to the death before succumbing.

A struggle is a scene… a scene is attention… attention attracts the Administration… Administration is forced to respond… the response is to remove the player from the Game…. Type A's want to play.

I have seen the Boa Constrictor style of dominance in action.

It's not pretty.

The slow steady squeeze that ultimately brings a man to his knees and finally to a level that no one should ever reach. The recipient will either check himself into Protective Custody or commit suicide.

The later preferred by many.

I come in at six three, buck ninety five. I don't believe the word pussy has ever come up when I was the topic of the conversation, certainly never when I was present. I am a staunch supporter of justice. I don't start fights, prefer to reason it out, however, if you feel that it's the only manner in which our differences can find resolve… I'll accommodate.

The problem is as follows… I am about to not celebrate my forty second birthday –versus - young bangers in their mid-twenties that spend their leisure at the pile, a bunch of leisure.

Did I mention that there were three of them?

I don't want to fuck with this, leave me alone, let me fly under the radar and complete my sentence. I want a chance to put the pieces of my self-destructed life back together when this is over.

Reasonable space… that is all I ask.

About a week later, electing not to go to the cattle trough, I was laying on my bunk reading when I felt the presence…

"Hey white boy… what you got for us?"

I looked over to see my favorite three pricks, in the same positions as before.

"Get the fuck outa here, asshole"
"Oooh… an old man with attitude… come on man, just give us some store and we'll get out of here. You know… like some soap, chips, stamps, candy bars. Something"
"Get your fucking ass outa my house"

The spokesman looked back at spotter dude to make sure the all clear was still on.

I thought about all the pain I was about to experience.

"Let me see what kinda store you got"

He opened my locker to help himself to my stuff.

Please dear Lord don't let this hurt too much.

I launched myself from my top bunk perch, maybe seven feet from where spokesman stood. He had glanced back at spotter dude just as I sprang so when he looked back at me my forehead was about two inches from the bridge of his nose.

Here you go, STORE that homie.

It sounded like the thump you hear when you do a knuckle freshness check on a melon at the market.

I sure hope he jacked some cotton balls at his last stop for his soon to be VERY bloody nose.

Just before my lights went out I had heard a very loud and a very clear "AAAAH FUUUUCK"

I needed to go to the bathroom but I couldn't move, my right leg and hand seemed to be stuck and I couldn't figure out what the problem was.

"Don't try to move, we're almost done here, do you know where you are?"

Of course I know where I'm at...

"Yah... I'm at uh.......uh"

Why don't I know where I'm at?

"I'm....uh...
"Don't try to talk anymore, you're in the Infirmary. You were in a fight. Right now I'm finishing stitching up your cheek and you've got a cracked cheekbone"
"I need to go to the bathroom"
"I'll bring in a bedpan, I don't want you to move until I can do a thorough check on you, besides your ankle and wrist are cuffed to the bedrails"
"Could you bring it in... I really need to go"

As I gained my wits he returned with the bedpan...

"So what happened in there, were those guys trying to Jack you?"
"Nah, we just had a little disagreement Doc, that's all"
"Well it was a hell of a disagreement that you both lost, he got seven stitches and a broken nose"
"Good"

After spending an extra day in the Infirmary, recuperating and having to confirm numerous times to numerous inquisitions that it was only a disagreement and not a Jack, I was wheeled into the Disciplinary wing of the prison, the Hole.

I had only one headlight and one hellava headache. My left lamp was also a little swollen, so looking around wasn't an option.

From what I could determine there wasn't much to see anyway. A six by six cinder block room with a stainless steel toilet and matching sink, one caged-in light bulb.

The steel door had a slot in it.

It was impossible to tell how much time had passed or whether it was daytime or some hour in the night. The slot in the door would slide open and a tray of food would appear. A voice would say "grab it" as it continued its journey inside, if you didn't grab it in time, it crashed to the floor.

The slot would then click shut.

I had asked for a doctor at one point, but didn't receive an answer.

A while later the doctor showed up.

The only other sounds you could hear was an occasional scream of...

"Let me outa here","Hey Honkies, God Damn it", "In here you muuuthaaafuuuuckeeeers,"Cracker,yooumuuuthaaafuuuuckeee", "gimmee a cigarette muuuthaaafuuuuckeeers"

Once in a while you could hear someone crying.

It wasn't pleasant.

On the last visit the doctor had made he told me that it was Thursday, I had been there for six days.

Glancing at his watch I noticed that it was three o'çlock.

"Doc, I'm having problems knowing how long I have slept or even figuring out if I should be sleeping at whatever hour it maybe, would you tell me if it is daytime or nightime right now"
"It is early in the morning"

I had just eaten what I thought was my dinner about a half of an hour before he arrived. They must play with the timing of the food so you don't have a clue what hour or even day it is.

I can't say for sure, maybe seven meals later, I heard a voice...

"Hey, old man, you got some fuck'n balls"

I didn't know if that comment was directed at me, but the voice sure sounded familiar.

"Yo, white boy... you broke my fucking nose"

I didn't say anything. The voice sounded like it was coming from a couple cells down and across the way.

It must have been a busy weekend because there were a lot more sounds... clanging doors, rattling keys and of course, screaming and yelling. Some even were still trying to settle their disputes.

Things certainly livened up.

... "Yo, homie, talk to me. YO, white boy from Unit A, talk to me muthafuka"

I just listened.

... "You broke my damn nose, that was a good one Home Slice, bet ya can't do that again, just you and me. Straight up"
"Fuck you"
"Hey, the Cracker speaks"
"Fuck you Prick"
"Ah man... why you want to be like that, we just came by to say hello... you know, like the welcome committee"
"Fuck you dude"
"Why you be like that, see what happened, you got us all thrown in the Hole"

"YOU got us thrown in here, you fuck"
"You're a LA boy, aren't you? I can tell by the way you're talk'n"

I didn't answer, there were keys coming down the hall.

Spokesman also shut up.

After I had eaten my breakfast at lunchtime or dinner for yesterdays lunch or lunch for tomorrows breakfast... who knows, they came around and collected the trays and sporks.

I had just finished my five sets of one hundred push-ups after every meal program, a jump start to the SSIIJ6Y plan and was just about to settle in on my very comfortable floor and start reading the book I finally snagged off the "Once-a-week" book cart and gossip agency...

"Yo, white boy... what chu doing?"

I ignored him.

"Ah, come on old man, talk to me"
"What the fuck, you step into my house without an invite and screw me up for a while, now you want to have a friendly fucking conversation?"
"Don't take it personal homie, it's just business. We had to check on ya. Like, make sure you know what's up"
"Yah, I know what's up, you came in to Jack me"
"Hey, hey... not so loud"
"Fuck you man... I know the god-damn rules"
"Yah, I heard you said we just had a disagreement... good look'n "

I didn't respond.

The next morning I heard the doctor talking to someone and then…

"Ah man… that fuck'n hurt!!"

I coughed out a very clear…

"PUSSY"

I couldn't resist saying it, but I sure didn't want a one on one with that fire plug, it was just one of those Had To's.

"It'll be tender for another week or so, you know the drill, this isn't your first"
"Yah, all right Doc. Hey, before you leave, you got some tobacco?"
"Can't give you any even if I did Jerome… you should quit anyway"

As he passed outside my door he stopped…

"You doing alright in there Frieze?"
"Yes, doing just fine Doc… not hurt at all, not a scratch. Thank you"

Another Had To.

I heard the far away clank of a door shutting.

It got real quiet for a little while and I had been deep in thought…

"I know you're from So Cal, which school you go to… I did SC"

"Listen Jerome, I really don't feel like having a conversation with you, why don't you talk with your two Homies that came in with you on your visit"

"Ah man, don't be call'n me that… anyway, they be gone for a long time, only had to do five. You know, they didn't have a disagreement with anybody, they just tried to get you off me"

"Jesus Christ"

"Listen… you just tell me what school you went to in LA and I won't bother you no more"

"I didn't go to college"

"You sure… you sound educated to me, you know… kinda smart"

"Well dude, if I'm so god damn smart, what in the fuck am I doing sitting in this cell… in Prison, having this conversation with you?"

He was true to his word… the extent of our conversation from that point on was the occasional… "You do'n alright white boy?" and my… "I'm do'n just fine black boy"

About twenty or so meals later my door opened and a guard announced…

"Let's go Frieze, vacation's over. Time to go see the world"

As I exited I looked down the hall in the direction where I had thought spokesman's voice had been coming.

He was stepping through his door into the hallway, our eyes met up and he got a big smile and nodded… like we were old friends.

Are you kidding me?

What a crazy God damn world I've just stepped into.

Once we got outside and into the sunlight we were allowed a few minutes to let our eyes adjust.

After our escorts deemed that we had had enough time to acclimate ourselves, the march to Unit A commenced.
No eye contact, no conversation.

Once inside he went left, I went right.

Behind me I could hear his homies welcoming him home...

"T-bone... you out! Yo, check this out nigga......"

I didn't get any... "Welcome home Scotty". In fact, it was open pod time, where most of the convicts were outside of their cells playing Pi-nuc, dominos or watching TV. Many of which turned around and looked at me like I was lost.

As I walked up to my cell door and was just about to open it I noticed that there was a towel hanging. This meant one of two things, Frank was either taking a crap or he was on a date... with one of his palms. I quickly jammed myself into reverse and sat down on the stairs about ten feet away. I figured I'd be there at least fifteen minutes after he took the towel down from the slotted window. I didn't need any whiffs or in the other case, didn't care to see his face expressing the contentment of afterglow.

I sat there taking in the sights when Sling came up...

"Hey bro, we got your back man. It's already in the makes. We'll get them fucking niggers"

Now, I've never been an advocate for using the N word, in fact I usually admonish the person using it in my presence. This time however, I thought I would skip the reprimand, it probably wasn't the best time or place to debate the issue.

"Listen... Sling, don't do anything on my account, I'm satisfied with the outcome"

"We can't just let it be, they went into the wrong neighborhood. They can't do that. That got everybody on point, all the shot callers are hav'n a meeting about what to do"

Great, I've been here for just a little over two months, half of which has been spent in the Hole.

Now, I'm at the forefront of a Race riot.

I had witnessed what happens when racial tension gets stirred up, over at CCA. It's not fun and has a long lasting effect on everybody. The Agitator is usually the primary target, if nothing more than to set an impressionable example.
Daaamn, I've got another six years of THIS??

"Listen bro, I took pretty good care of the dude that came in, I don't think he'll be walking in on me anymore. Let's just let everything settle for a while"
"It don't matter what we want… the callers got it now. What they decide is what's go'n down"

I didn't know how long it had been since Frank removed the towel, but I didn't want any more conversation. Four showers in the last month was not enough to ever feel clean, especially since they were ice cold and tough to stay under.

When I walked in I didn't notice any foul smell and without thinking I looked at Frank when he said "Howdy". Daaaaamn, he was all content. Shit. That'll fuck up my brain for a while.

For the next couple of days I kept a pretty good vigilance on my three sixty, I heard various versions on what took place.

Because there were three of them in my cell, the truth be known.

I was called in to talk with the Shot Caller of the Peckerwoods.

Mountain was a most appropriate handle for this lug. I'm talk'n huge… maybe six seven, three eighty. If I'm wrong it's because I under estimated.

Mountain was a surprisingly mild mannered fellow. I was glad to see that that was what he chose at the personality counter, I'm sure he could have had his pick of any of the wide range of manners on the menu.

He asked me to give him a re-play, which I did. You don't lie to the guy that's controlling your protection, especially when you're the new guy on the minority squad.

The big boy made up for a lot, but the guys in white only covered about ten percent of the population.

It was explained to me that the guy I landed on, T-bone, was the shot caller for the blacks. He was on a training mission for the guy at his side. I was supposed to be an easy target, being an old man and all.

After all the smoke settled an agreement was reached.

Apparently a trade for a previous altercation or for a soon to go down altercation was negotiated. The fact that T-Bone suffered personal injury during an easy target training mission put his stature in jeopardy.

I was pleased that there wasn't a retaliatory strike due to the incident and jumped right back into the… just let me fly under the radar frame of mind.

Seeing about twelve of my weekly paychecks I decided that SSIIJ6Y plan would be a more beneficial way to spend the next... a little less than six years, at FCI Tucson. I told Rudy that it had been a pleasure working for him and then headed off to inform Lt. Smiley of my decision.

He tried to talk me out of it but once I told him that my decision was final he told me that during our conversation he had also made a final decision. He turned on his heels, grabbed the radio off his waist rack and summoned three of his comrades. Upon their arrival I was unceremoniously cuffed and lead to my awaiting suite in the Hole.

Ah Jesus, not this again.

If this keeps up they may have to put my name on the door. Scotty, my man... what happened to flying under the radar?

After about eight or nine meals my door was opened and I was informed that the Warden wanted to speak with me. I was allowed to take a very rapid shower and have a quick shave, and then I was lead to the Wardens office.

As soon as I walked in he took one look at me and said...

"My God, get this man a damp towel".

I didn't know what he was talking about until the towel arrived and he told me to tap my face with it. The first tap was sufficient in cluing me in...

"Ah, I think I wacked as many goose bumps as I did whiskers"

The Warden got a pretty hearty laugh out of my comment, I'm sure he knew about the refrigerated water that spewed from the shower heads in the Hole. The mental picture of someone trying to shave after getting out was rather humorous.

After thinking about what I said, I even started to laugh. Soon, even the two guards that accompanied me started to laugh, the more blood I wiped off, the funnier it got.

… "Alright everybody"

He started to chuckle again and I noticed that for him to continue speaking he needed to walk around his office, not looking in my direction.

"What is this about you refusing to work, Mr. Frieze?"

He looked back at me and coughed out a quick laugh… he quickly diverted his eyes.

"Sir, I am not refusing to work, I just want to make sure that I use this time-out in my life to improve myself, personally. Educate myself. I'll need every advantage that I can gain to re-enter society with a fighting chance to live out my years in relative comfort. I'll be almost fifty years old when I leave here. Starting all over again is frightening to me"
"You can't do that and work?"
"It's a little disheartening when you put in forty plus hours of work into your week and look at the sixty cents you earned. If I applied the same forty hours to educating myself, I could leave here a freak'n Brain Surgeon"
"We don't have medical training material here… do we?"

He looked over at one of the guards who just answered with a shrug.

POOR EXAMPLE

"All I'm saying is that if you have a job that is half of the hours, I could spend the other half of the day working on my Scotty's self-improvement in just 6 years plan"

"Your what? Ah never mind, anybody that is trying to plan for their future is good by me. I like your attitude Mr. Frieze, I wish I had another eleven hundred guys that thought like you. I'll tell you what, today is Friday, I'm going to have you released from the Disciplinary Unit. You are to have one of the guards escort you to this office at one in the afternoon, next Wednesday. I'll make sure your Command Center is aware of this. I want you to have a proposal for me on what you could do for work and NOT upset the applecart. If it appears to ANYONE that I am playing favoritism it will not be good for YOU or ME. Our discussion has given me a couple of ideas on ways to motivate some of our inmates that have real potential but have settled on the comforts of being institutionalized"

"Thank you, I'll come up with something"

"The other reason that I'm releasing you from Detention is that I don't want to be liable should you bleed to death attempting to shave in there again"

He started in with his hearty laugh again as he gave the guards a hand gesture dismissing us all.

The following Wednesday I was escorted to the Wardens office where he accepted my proposal. Officially freed up to put the SSIIJ6Y Plan into full gear.

I was excited to get underway and now actually optimistic for my chances to recapture a normal life after Prison.

I started my new job keeping all the windows clean in the Chow hall, laundry, commissary and visitation center.

The first few months I cleaned and polished each window which took me half of a day. I left the house at seven in the morning, my goal was to be home to begin my hour workout immediately after the lunch siren.

After a <u>warm</u> shower I would study all I could find and all my family could send me on the starting of a small business, starting with how to put together a business plan, annual projections and accounting.

My secondary interest was to be fluent in Spanish.

This was important for the success of the SSIIJ6Y Plan.

I figured I could take classes at U of A while completing my mandatory five years of Intense Probation, the provision to my sentence that Christopher Hyman insisted on in lieu of appealing Judge Goldstein's verdict.

Of the few vacations that I had taken in my life, the most enjoyable were always South of the Border. In fact, as far south of the border as one could get on the Baja Peninsula. I liked that little town on the tip... Cabo San Lucas.

Whenever I had visited there the locals always treated me as if it were my home town.

The one thing I noticed or I should say didn't notice was with all the vehicles down there I couldn't spot a place to service them. I'm not talking about mechanics... there were plenty of those. I'm talking about the rapid servicing of the fluids... Oil and filter change.

A Jiffy Lube type operation.

It was totally foreign (excuse the pun) to them. I had asked around on my last trip and the only way to get your oil changed was to make an appointment with your favorite mechanic and hope he wasn't too busy. Even if he wasn't it seemed to take at least half of a day by the time he checked the auto parts stores for your favorite brand and the best price.

My retirement plan had always been to move to Mexico when I hit fifty five years old... there is no reason to alter that. I can still achieve it, even with this detour that I have created for myself. It certainly gave me hope for my future and something to occupy my mind during the times the Prison was on lockdown.

I had reduced the hours it took me to keep the windows clean. I started with determining which ones needed daily attention, the number one's, then assigned a number to each window, the number five's only needing to be cleaned once a week.

This system allowed me to work-out and study earlier.

I found time to get outside more often and to relax by playing cards in the evening with a group of under the radar kind of guys.

Pinochle was an interesting card game, which I got the hang of pretty quick.

We bet stamps, the Universal Prison Monetary Exchange for card games, football bets, Saturday burritos at the soccer field and all the self-proclaimed mini markets.

There were a couple of 7-11's located in every pod.

Each with their own specialty;
Cell 235 had all the sweets... candy, doughnuts, sodas etc.
Cell 101 had the supply of beans, cheese, tortillas and Cup-a-Soup.

Any entrepreneur could hang out a shingle; the permits were issued and monitored by the shot callers.

The Guards didn't need to pack a lunch, if they knew how and when to look away.

There were the Pisto stores, eraser cap of weed stores, dime paper of H stores, tattoo shops and the more popular than you would think stop-off... for those that didn't have a towel to hang or just wanted to cheat on their palms.

All accepting stamps and open till 10 pm lockdown.

When a store had too many complaints, poor business practice or just pissed somebody off, the cell mysteriously went up in flames the next day while un-occupied.

The official report would always determine that the cause of the fire was due to an unattended smoldering cigarette.

It was a well-functioning society... sometimes screwed up because a guard didn't get his free Crusty Crumb or a Caller got snubbed in one of the stores.

Otherwise, a necessary and very well maintained system.

Each cell has two folding chairs assigned to its occupants, well stenciled with the cell number. The chair is considered an extension of the house and no matter where it is placed on the prison grounds. it cannot be touched, moved, tampered with or God forbid... sat in, by anyone other than the owner.

To do so is an insult and is considered the same no-no as it would be if you walked into someone's cell, slid into their bunk and accidentally pee'd yourself while taking a nap.

Touching someone's chair was the number one most popular reason for a fistfight... just beating out the non-payment of drug or gambling debts.

The Titanic… the highly touted, just released, mega movie was coming to FCI Tucson and the troops were excited… including Scotty. That's right, I wanted to see the stupid boat movie, as Frank had put it. The last movie I had seen was Charlie's Angels at movie night in CCA. The showing, almost two years ago, still stands as the All-time towel hang record holder for a single night feature. I didn't expect Titanic to challenge the record, I just have always been intrigued by that tragic event. I hoped it had some historical accuracy, maybe some actual footage. I hadn't even seen previews.

Movie day morning I was ready at 4:55 am with chair in hand, just waiting to hear the electronic click of my cell door lock.

At precisely 5:00:01 AM, when the door popped, I planned to race to the movie room and select the most primo spot there to view this state of the art masterpiece. Frank didn't want to go because there was always a fight breaking out in the movie room.

I normally didn't go for the same reason. There was always someone talking too much, farting too much, spilling something on somebody or throwing stuff in the darkness.

Always something, but I figured this movie was different, EVERYBODY is going to want to see this in its entirety, nobody is going to create havoc, they'll miss something.

CLACK… I was off, there were a handful of others headed for the same finish line.

A bunch of wannabe in front for the movie dudes were coming from the two upper tiers.

My cell was on the main floor, no problem, I even slowed my pace and started to meander so I could watch the mad dash. I had such an advantage I even thought about doing a little moon walk'n… just to clown ém.

These guys were bump'n and clang'n all the way down the four sets of stairs. They were log jam'n on the turn backs, then an all out sprint across the tier to the next set of stairs.

The pod had an ingress/egress system of staircases that were designed so that if half of the pod was under siege they could still access the tier above or below the troubled area.

The problem with this design is that if you are in a hurry… like maybe a fire broke out, you'd have a pretty good crisp go'n on by the time you made it to the ground level.

Ah well, that's alright… let's try out the design anyway, they're just a bunch of criminals in that building for Christ sakes.

Just as I had cleared the common area and was the first with my hand on the movie room door, I looked back in time to see a late riser, Jorge Durán, chuck his chair from the third tier, probably thinking the dash down the staircase would be faster unencumbered. Two seconds after the chair hit ground level, so did the sleeping Sergeant Lee in the Command Center.

I'm pretty sure that JD, the brain child of the chair launch, will be looking at a caged light bulb tonight instead of the Mega movie.

I placed my chair about the 30 yard line and over on the right hash mark. I don't like to be on top of the screen or directly in the middle. Plus I'd like to keep these boys in my peripheral.

The room filled up with chairs in about an hour.

I was ready for a good movie and a mental escape for three hours.

The under the radar boys decided to have a Titanic Pinochle Tournament. I wanted to attend both of them, however the decision was easy, there will always be another Pi-nuc tournament.

At about 6:45pm I headed over to the movie room so I could check out the crowd. It wasn't so bad… I think some of the diehard Pi-nuc players noticed the books of stamps stacking up at the other Titanic debut and decided to abandon ship. :-]

I couldn't see my chair, there were a group of Norteños or Sureños or Ese's or Chilangos or Paisas or Chicanos sitting in a circle, the center of which was right about where I had last seen my prized possession.

Ah shit… not again.

How many racial groups do I need to go through?? I sure hope the Mexican's are going to exchange information after this, I reeaaally don't feel like pain right now.

As I approached all conversation ceased.

There weren't a set of eyeballs not on me.

Of course, the hombre with the most ink and the biggest guns was comfy in my chair. I looked towards the exit one last time to see if maybe the guard would be where he was supposed to be.

Nope, diversion hombre was doing his job muy bien.

"You're in my chair"
"Oh yah Güero… I no espeeka english"

His fan club thought that was the funniest thing that they have ever heard.

I looked directly into the eyes of some of the idiots that were laughing the hardest. They diverted their glances downward immediately, the ass kissing pussies. Then I slapped my thigh and joined in on the laughter with equal enthusiasm.

Not having fun anymore, I abruptly stopped laughing and looked back at Señor No Espeeka English…

"Get the fuck outta my chair"
"Oh, si,si Gabacho… after the pínche movie is over, Pendejo"

I hit him in the side of his head real hard… an absolute direct hit on his ear. I had shifted my body weight with the punch to ensure that it had everything in my arsenal.

He toppled to the floor like a gunnysack full of wet tortillas.

There was a frozen moment in time, like someone clicked pause.

My quick response was a surprise to everyone present. I really don't know why… maybe they were expecting an intelligent debate.

I threw a punch to my left and missed my intended target, whatever that was, it just seemed like the thing to do.

The pummeling commenced.

… "Hey, how have you been Doc… it's been a while"

"Mr. Frieze, it has been a while, I had hoped you weren't going to be a frequent customer"

"Doc… come on, it's been like… almost two years since I've popped in for a visit"

"Wait a minute... I just saw you, like a month ago"

"Doc… tooth aches don't count, come on dude… that's not fair"

While having my tooth looked at we had a pretty good conversation. Both of us having shared our brief history's and the How & Why we had ended up here. It seemed that he had had an interesting life. After a couple turn of events, let's just call them hiccups, in his professional life this was the only place he could get a job.

His resume was quite impressive.

The three hours it took for the fifteen minute procedure to repair my tooth was indicative to our mutual enjoyment of the conversation.

A rarity on these premises.

"Was it another disagreement Frieze?"

"Yes sir… evidently a staunch difference in opinions, same as before"

We both chuckled and shook our heads in false bewilderment.

This time the damage was limited to multiple small bone fractures in my right hand and swelling on my left eye and forehead.

After a catch-up on what's been happening in both of our lives he opened the door where two guards were anxiously awaiting the opportunity to present me with matching bracelets.

… "Yeow… whooa, come on Sarge… easy on the right paw"

"Sorry Frieze"

It's funny how the passage of time manipulates, in which the result dictates your current state of being. I don't want to get all freaky on you, but the exchange between the Sarge and I struck me.

Four years ago it was Inmate Frieze and Sergeant Martinez.

An apology not even remotely considered.

Some of the relations had remained the same, there were quite a few of the Guards that shouldn't be allowed to exit. The only reason they aren't assigned their own cell is because they don't have the balls to commit the crime that compels them. They are working here so they can be as close to the criminal element as possible, a vicarious fulfillment without the personal risk. Others are just wannabe cops that can't get past the physical and/or mental tests that are required from the various agencies.

The criminal wannabes are easy to get along with, they are jealous.

The wannabe cops are the assholes.

They press their advantage in every situation, evidently for no reason other than because they are in a dangerously unwarranted authoritative position to do so. Right or wrong has no bearing on the matter.

In fact the later is preferred, even relished, to further highlight the power bestowed upon them.

Pure pussy pieces of shit... do I need to expound.

… "Hey Doc, drop by for a visit if you're in the neighborhood… you know, check on my hand. I believe you know where my suite is located"

"Yah, I probably will, your place is pretty easy to spot… it has the plaque screwed to the door with Mr. Frieze on it, doesn't it?"

I laid there on that ice cold concrete floor thinking about the progress I'd been making on the SSIIJ6Y plan, I was quite satisfied. I hadn't deviated any and am right on course. I was right about at the halfway mark of completing my sentence. It was hard to believe that I have been in prison for just going on four years.

I drifted off to one of my other favorite pastimes… OBE.

I have become a voracious reader. Every night, except for the occasional Pi-nuc tournament, I am reading… Fiction, Non-Fiction, Thrillers, Sci-fi, Western's, Biography's and Autobiography's… all the way to Medical Journals.

Anything and everything I can get my hands or eyes on.

One book that I took a special interest in was "The Out of Body Experience"

Before I get into my explanation of OBE, I want to make a qualifying statement: The fact that I have been in prison for four years, under extreme duress, has not altered the pattern in which my marbles fire. A comprehensive marble inventory is initiated immediately upon the closing of the previous, which has been an ongoing practice since my first night in the fish bowl.

To date, all my marbles are accounted for and functioning properly.

Alright… back to my OBE experiments.

After reading up on the subject and in particular, reading The Out Of Body Experience, I decided to give it a shot… nothing half assed, I really tried. The result was that I felt a little of what they said would be the outcome.

On Scotty's rating scale from 5-10; with 10 being the best… I gave it a 3.

A few weeks later… on the second day of a three day lock-down due to racial tension, I thought I'd give it another try.

I reviewed the process, following it to the letter. I laid on my back, intertwined my fingers and placed my hands just below the sternum, concentration was my only task.

I tried to recall our adventure down to the most minute detail. An excursion that my brothers and I enjoyed when we all got new bicycles for Christmas.

Starting by breathing slowly, taking in the maximum amount of air until reaching lung capacity, released it gently through my nostrils until my lungs were completely void of the inhalation.

As I started to repeat this process if necessary--------

My body lurched from the prone position with such force that it woke Frank up from his nap in the lower bunk.

"What in the hell was that?"
"Sorry bro, didn't mean to wake you up…"

I remembered looking at the clock just before I started the breathing exercise… 3:10 in the afternoon. It was now 3:50.

I felt as if I had only closed my eyes for a few moments.

Wow… I went there, I was there again!!

My brothers and I were at the Swamp once again, riding our bikes through the trees, the whoop d' whoops, chasing each other along the winding up and downs where the drainage from the surrounding streets collected and formed our "River". Tim was chasing Mike, Greg chasing Headward, Jerry, Kevin, Kenny. Little Scotty was parked under a tree watching, just learning to fly under the radar.

It was the only patch of raw land in our neighborhood.

There weren't any places that the kids on summer break could ride their bikes with reckless abandon other than the Swamp.

It was also a necessary detour on our way to Lambert Little League practice.

Anyone over the age of 10 would tell you that it resembled nothing even close to a Swamp. When you're 7 years old and the only other choice is the maze of LA streets and alleys, the Swamp was created from our vivid imaginations.

To the 20 or so neighborhood kids that played there every weekend when school was in session, every day in the summer, that was exactly what it was… what we saw. Two square blocks of adventure… willow trees with branches that hung to the ground lining the three foot wide river, six foot if a branch fell from a tree just right. A couple of us would dismount our Schwinns and help the branch find the right location, if Mother Nature missed the target.

A chorus of Whoop'n and Holler'n stirred a pot of courage in every participant's belly.

Displays of bravado were mimicked by the younger as the treacherous double back came into view. The attempt at jumping over the newest danger was the last obstacle in our quest to escape the villainous and monstrously dangerous Swamplands of East Los Angeles.

The vision, still vividly fresh in my mind when I awoke, allowed me the continued enjoyment throughout that night.

I am now saying to you all... I <u>went</u> there. I heard the voices once again, saw the freckles on the faces of my brothers, felt the rocky path beneath the tires and smelled the fresh summer air of Los Angeles 1961... That's right, fresh.

Without a doubt an unequaled and most enjoyable experience.

On Scotty's scale from 5-10; with 10 being the best, I gave it a 19.

On the first day of my third invitation to stay in the All Inclusive Castigatory Suites at the FCI Resort in Tucson, Arizona, I chose to go visit my Grandmother Genevleve at her apartment, just off Little Santa Monica.

I heard her voice coming from the kitchen. Whatever she was cooking smelled so good my mouth started watering. I could hear the tick-tock coming from the old wind up Elgin on the apartment's fireplace mantle.

I wanted to play on the fire escape but in Grandmas gentle speech... "No, No Scotty that's too high and very dangerous, come on in here and help Grandma stir the gravy"

When I awoke on the floor in the Hole I could hear myself repeating, as would a child… "I'm sorry Grandma… I'm sorry Grandma"

Once I gained full consciousness the words ceased. I felt <u>true</u> sadness. I still had the scent of her cooking in my nostrils.

I wiped my face with my hands to rid myself of the grog hangover and found tears running down my cheeks. I sat on the floor, without moving, in an emotional state somewhere between utter amazement and freaked the fuck out.

When the food tray started on its journey through the food slot I yelled "No thanks" and watched it retreat until it disappeared. By the time the next tray began its journey I had already resumed the prone position, however my wide eyed gaze on the ceiling hadn't diminished a millimeter.

I want to quickly jump to approximately six months after this incident, which is about how long it took for me to not be obsessed with it on a daily basis.

My final journey however, did leave me with a lingering question that I would like to present afterwards.

Scotty's OBE's will then be laid to rest.

I decided to journey just once more, to visit my first neighborhood and see my childhood friends. Our family moved from this home when I had been eight years old.

I could feel the fresh cut grass in our front lawn under my feet, it's savored aroma a bygone treat, sat in the Rammey's new Silver 57' Nomad Wagon. Two door with black, silver and red trimmed seats, some kind of "Anniversary model".

I saw the Lairitz family again. Stood once again on the red brick planter by the front door, ready to scare the hell out of the next person to exit.

I even noticed that the 6 in the brass numerals 13561, which had been nailed to one of the posts on our porch depicting the address, was missing the bottom brass nail.

I played on the side lawn again with Karen, the girl next door that came into this world two days after I had entered. She was my best friend and the first girl that showed me her underwear. It had been my request when she asked me what I wanted for my seventh birthday.

It was a great and final journey.

There is a sense, an emotional response that our body's alarm system will emit from way deep inside that is triggered by the thought of an event of epic proportions.

This feeling is like none other.

Some refer to it as coming from the "Pit of their Stomach"

As of this writing I have not as yet heard anyone come even remotely close to an appropriate description of that feeling.

We have all felt it.

It's that deep feeling we get after the thought of a catastrophic event in our life that permanently alters the axis in which our body and/or mind are accustomed. The thought of being responsible for altering someone else's life will cause the alarm. Inadvertently causing great harm to someone or something will trigger it.

The thought of a monumental loss will cause the sense. You know the feeling... right?

What's my point?

Thinking about that evening when I awoke on the floor from visiting with my Grandmother triggers that emotional sense. It emits from my very core, stronger than I have ever felt that "Pit in the Stomach" attention getter before.

There is not a stronger sense of reality than this very moment, I mean this very moment... damn.
OK... are you ready? THIS VERY MOMENT... shit, it's gone also.

OK, let me try putting it this way... You are convinced that you got back this morning from your vacation in Hawaii.
When you arrived it IS reality... right now it WAS reality.

I am equally convinced that I journeyed to those selected locations and somehow re-visited reality. It scared the hell out of me when I got back from Grandma's house.

The thought of it scares the shit out of me now.

I don't know if my experience was the intended result of the OBE exercise or not. There is one thing I do know for sure... it was a catastrophic event that altered Scotty's axis.

Alright, now for my lingering question...

When I visited my old neighborhood, what would have happened if I had asked Karen to show me her underwear again and the cops showed up? Reality is that I'm a middle-aged man, however reality at the time I made the request was that I am only seven years old.
Would I be tried as an adult or as a minor?

Whooooa… I just read the last four pages I wrote on the OBE part of my life.

God damn it Don… this was your freakin fault.

My good buddy Don pops in to check on my progress in the writing of this masterpiece and either says… "You aren't done yet??" or "You need to fill it in with more stories, fluff it up… embellish a little"

You know what?? I'm going to leave all this crapola in the book.

When Don reads what the result of his suggestions produced he will be down to being a one comment kind of kibitzer next time he pops in.

You think I kicked that mule around the room enough times?

To you all… I promise to take the fluff and embellishment folders, along with my OBE mule and chuck'em out the back door… right next to the dead horse.

Oh yah… and no more spark'n while I'm writ'n anymore.

I just got back from taking a break, as you could see I was getting a little pissy with all that fluff crap throwing me sideways. But you know what? I had a brilliant idea just now.

If this turns out to be less than the masterpiece I promised… I'm blam'n DON!! God damn guy is out there golfing every day, I'm in here stressing over this book, trying to recall exactly the way things went down, trying to be fairly accurate.

If the book is a failure… DON'S FAULT.

If it turns out to be successful....

"Thank you everybody, thank you, it was nothing. I did however, almost blow it by putting in too much fluff, but thank you very much"

I am C-O-V-E-R-E-D !!!----------FLUFF THAT DON.

Ok, back to the story...

It's my first night back in the Hole for punching out Señor No Espeeka English But I Drop Off To Sleep Pretty Fast At The Movies, for sitting in my chair.

The next morning Doc showed up to check on my hand and to give me some pain pills. He must of known that I would need them. I couldn't sleep because my hand was hurting so bad.

He also brought me a pillow, a couple of cigarettes, matches and a Granddaddy Snickers bar.

Doc jumped up to #1 on my Cool Dude list with that Snickers.

I asked him what had happened with Señor name is too long to repeat again.

"Last time I saw him they were putting him into a van to transfer him to Victorville, his third fight in four months. I don't know what you hit him with, but when I did a last check on him before the van took off he was still having a problem focusing. I'm also pretty sure that his bells were still ringing"
"Hopefully it made him bi-lingual again"

They opened my door after only three days....

"Frieze, try to refrain from hitting everybody that looks at you wrong"

I started to plead my case... save your breath Scotty.

The next year flew by, myself and two other wannabe Señores were studying Spanish three days a week. My sister had been sending me the workbooks from the University in Ashland, Oregon.

We had just cracked the workbook to begin on our third semester.

My business plan, complete with start-up costs, building costs, five year projections etc. was taking shape and I had already moved into the visualizing stage.

I was quite satisfied with the progression.

I have been told that I am a "Big Dreamer"

Well, I was thoroughly enjoying the Big Dreaming, it was keeping my mind well occupied when trying to fall asleep a night and well off that ever so illusive "End of the tunnel", which was starting to illuminate.

Everything was on cruise control until one morning when I was summoned to the Lt's office...

"Good morning Frieze... hey, I need your help. We always have an annual inspection around this time. The inspectors will be here first thing tomorrow morning. It's always a surprise inspection, but this year we didn't get the tip off. Anyway, we are going to come get you after lockdown, would you do a super clean-up on those windows in the bakery. There is an Inspector that has a pet peeve about bakery windows... fuck'n idiot, I think he's already marked the deduction before he even arrives. I want to get his ass this year... can you help me?"

There were a bunch of guards that I would have paid a lot to have this golden opportunity to say... Nah.

Lt. wasn't one of them...

"No problem Lt."
"Great, one of the guards will come get you around midnight... alright?"
"I'll be ready"
"You need anything?"
"Key's to the front door would be cool"
"I wish I could give ém to ya"

At 12:10 I heard the keys coming so I jumped off the bunk and took the two steps to our front door where I waited.

The quietest time here was normally between 11 pm – 3 am. In those hours the guards are accustomed to looking through the tiny cell windows for an unimpeded view of the two sleeping convicts. Knowing this and having a desire to fuck with somebody, you know, like when you feel like scaring the shit out of your sister just for the hell of it.

I pressed my face against the window, filling it border to border with my smashed down features.

The guards had a kind of look in, then twist the key habit, so there I waited.

True to form, he came in from the side fumbling with his keys, then turned and stuck his face in the window... without the glass it would have been a kiss.

He actually screamed.

As he was going backwards his ass kept getting closer to the floor as his legs were churning trying to regain the perpendicular with his body position.

The landing pad turned out to be about twenty feet into the dayroom.

I will give him a little credit, those legs of his gave it one hell of an effort.

The pod lit up with the emergency bright lights, three guards came running in and just about every cell window filled in with a face of the curious.

I was laughing so hard I had to unzip my pants FAST and just as I turned to the left the pee flew.

Thank God for that all in one room design.

The rescue guards were trying to be upset with me, but they couldn't come up with a justifiable reason, I was locked in my cell.

I couldn't speak. The second I started to gain a little composure the mental picture would flash and immediately I was totally, I mean TOTALLY incapacitated from laughter.

I'm still laughing.

At 12:40 I arrived at the bakery, the mental picture still screwing up my ability to complete a sentence.

It was just myself and one guard, a kind of semi ok dude. That's a high mark... I mean he's a god damn guard for Christ sake. Wilkes had been stitched on his shirt, so I guess he's Wilkes.

I had seen him around, however no interaction with him.

I'd never been in the Chow hall, bakery and the commissary building when it wasn't like an ant hill of activity. It was kind of spooky in that big ass kitchen when it's empty.

There were about six convicts working in a caged room.

We continued past them and finally stopped in the east corner of the building. I hadn't noticed that I walked past three large wire enforced glass windows. At a glance they looked like white stucco walls. He opened the door, then perused the interior before stepping aside allowing me to enter.

A quick survey of my task at hand told me that, by the amount of flour covering the windows, it was placed there by design. The bakers probably just wanted a little privacy; a swipe of my finger confirmed my suspicions.

I removed the butter encrusted flour off my finger, then I prepared a bucket full of my Mega Job Hyper-Turbo Super Solution.

Some people call it white vinegar and water... whatever.

It was a fairly easy job, with the room having a rolled up water hose that was hanging on a wall mounted bracket.

I discovered a three inch floor drain under one of the four by eight stainless steel tables.

The wall on the hallway side of the room had the 3 five by five windows and the door.

One of the tables was pushed up against the wall.

The height of the table was about two inches below the sill of the window. While placing my foot against the wall for a little leverage to move this monster of a table, I noticed a #10 can of something tucked in the corner of the room, well hidden by the four foot wide lower shelf of the table. I decided that I shouldn't be too hasty in moving the table into the center of the room. Perhaps the best manner in doing this job correctly would be to push the table along the wall and only away from the corner of the room.

Not too much, maybe to the edge of the door. I'd say... like no more than six inches. Ah yes, that will be perfect.

Initially I placed the bucket and large pile of rags under the window closest to the door, but after further review of the task, I thought maybe I should re-think my strategy.

After about two seconds of the back and forth mental debate, thoroughly weighing the pros vs. cons, I made a decision. Left to right is not correct... I should start in the corner.

One leg on the floor, the other laying on the table top V-style with the boys resting ever so comfortably on the edge of that cool stainless steel. I went to work on the window, while trying to hockey stick the can away from the corner with my size 13 prison issue steel toes.

The guard looked up from his tabloid.

I froze, my obviously contorted stance and the fact that I was starting this job bottom right hand corner going up tipped him off, damn it.

We just looked at each other for a couple of seconds….

"Big job, eh Frieze?"
"Sure is"

He went back to looking at the pictures.

No doubt which part of the entrance exams he failed.

I dropped the rag on top of the can. As I retrieved the rag I pulled the can away from the corner and pushed it back under the table. Curiosity was killing me, I knew that if somebody stashed it there it was something good.

I finished window one and was trying to figure out how to get to the can. I even threw out a couple "Man… I'm thirsty" in the wind.

Finishing window two at about the same time Wilkes flipped the tabloid to page two I acted like I was cleaning up a mess under the table, twisting the can so I could read the label.

OH   MY   GOD!! … My all time, number one, two & three most favorite dessert was right there… I even touched it.

I WILL figure out a way… IT'S MINE…

I had cleaned about 9/10 of window three and was starting to panic.

I was drooling in anticipation.

It has been six years since I have tasted this delectable treasure.

I have had many dreams in the last six years where it had made a cameo appearance.

I'm not leaving this room without it.

Suddenly Wilkes' body alarm went off on his radio. This particular signal means EVERYBODY to the rescue, officer in jeopardy. These boys take that one very seriously.

He leapt to his feet...

"Frieze, I'm locking you in"
"Thank you Jesus for your intervention, I promise that from now on I will go to church every Sunday, no more bad words…………….."

By the time he passed the last window I was already at the king sized commercial can opener that had been welded to the back table top, with #10 in hand.

I had spent a nano-second scanning the room for a spoon when I found my hand wrist deep into my treasure. As I was shoveling my sweet feast into my mouth with my skin scoop I was also trying to hip-check the table by the windows over to in front of the door.

I had lost my mind.

Nothing mattered.

I got enough of the table in front of the door to give me those few precious seconds, should Wilkes return rapidly, to do some turbo scoop'n.

When Wilkes finally returned, the #10 was laying sideways on the floor and so was I. He was a little freaked because of the table blocking the door and the fact that I couldn't get up to help move the table.

My stomach hurt to the touch. It was as taut as a basketball that it appeared I had swallowed.

After about five minutes of listening to Wilkes trying to coax me up to move the table, two guards came to the rescue and helped remove the obstruction. I was doubled up in such a ball that I didn't notice that one of the rescuers was Officer Backstroke, the guard that tried to kiss me through my cell window. When I finally recognized him my mind immediately provided me with a flash clip of the event, which got me into a laugh, pain, bigger laugh, greater pain cycle. I guess Backstroke also had a malfunction in his recollection circuitry.

They were all three standing there laughing and pointing at me, but when Backstroke finally recognized me, he lost it, his ability to speak followed suit.

Someone returned with a wheel chair in which I was placed and we all took off. Scotty and his three merry guard escort, they were all giggling throughout the trip to the Medical building.

To my surprise, Doc was seated behind his desk as Larry, Mo and Backstroke rolled me into his office. Doc looked up from his paperwork and pointed at me, slapped the top of his desk and started roaring in laughter, which got L, M & B started up again.

Backstroke came around from behind me, when I caught a glimpse of him a flash clip played and my funny/my pain cycle kicked in.

I found out why Backstroke had come around from behind me when the camera flashed in my eyes.

"Hey man... what's up with that"

Doc, still with a big grin on his face, opened a desk drawer and grabbed a small mirror...

"Easy Frieze... here, take a look"

It looked like I was in the first stage of one of those chick mud mask facials, except chocolate pudding was used instead of therapeutic mud.

Doc gave me some kind of chalky tasting white liquid that blew out my pipes within fifteen minutes. I was allowed to take a shower before being led to my suite.

I was deep in sleep, enjoying a sunny frolic on the beach with two senoritas that couldn't keep their hands off of me, when Lt's voice summoned me to the present...

"God damn..."
"God damn what Frieze? The warden wants to see you, but first I do, let's go... now"
"Alright already, may I wake up?"

Lt. looked back at the guard standing behind him...

"Bring Frieze to my office... twenty minutes"

Whew... that should give the ol'chubster enough time to deflate.

After I had been seated in front of Lt's desk for about ten minutes, he walked in, dismissed the guard and closed the door.

He was halfway between pissed off and jovial...

"Frieze, what the fuck, I ask you to do me a favor... which you did, very well by the way, then you create all kinds of havoc afterward. I should put you back in Disciplinary and leave you there until your time is up"

I just sat there looking at the front panel on his desk.

"Did you know that because you have already had three infractions that resulted in you having to be placed into Disciplinary Confinement that every day served thereafter has an additional penalty? Loss of Good Time"

"Holy shit Lt, I didn't know that one. Man… that's a big penalty in my book. Those days are important to me"

"Well, that bullshit last night cost you one so far, hope it was worth it"

"Yah… it was worth one, how many days am I going to lose?

"How many days do you think that bullshit was worth?"

"One"

He picked up the photo that Backstroke had taken in Doc's office, I didn't know that it was laying on the top of his desk. He looked at it for a moment, then looked at me…

"Fuck man… that IS funny, you're nut's Frieze"

He looked at the photo a little longer and started laughing pretty hard.

"I'm going to blow this up and frame it, it's go'n on my wall. That's fucking funny"

He handed it to me. I looked like a kid that did a full on face plant in a mud puddle.

I have to admit, it was pretty damn funny.

"Here on out, disciplinary will cost you a commensurate day of good time. The job you did for me last night helped give the kitchen the highest mark it has ever scored"

"I don't know what you did to those windows, but they were so clean it didn't even look like they had glass in them"

I thought… well, all you have to do is wash each one five times while you're stalling to find out what's in the #10 can.

If I would've washed them one more time there just may not of been any more glass in them.

"How many am I losing?"
"One. You're obviously an intelligent guy Frieze. Knock off this bullshit, do your time and get the hell out of here. You're short aren't you… like nineteen months?"
"Nineteen months, three weeks, four days and…"

I looked at the clock on his desk table…

"Twenty two hours, But hey Lt… who's counting"
"Slacker… get in here and get this guy outta my sight"

I snapped my glance back to Lt. with the - "Are you fucking kidding me, THAT'S his name?"- look on my face.

"And he is… now get outta here Frieze"

Slacker stepped in and just as we got to the door…

"Wait a minute Frieze you're not done yet, the Warden wants to see you. What in the hell else you been up to?"

Slacker's body alarm went off just as we had exited Lt's office so I was pushed into one of the emergency cells that each building in the compound had for exactly this purpose, where I remained for about three hours.

I finally started yelling for someone to open the goddamn door and let me out when a guard appeared and looked to be dumbfounded as to how I got in there. After another fifteen minutes or so Slacker showed up. He opened the door and we continued on to the Wardens office as if only 10 minutes had transpired since he put me in the stink'n place.

I'm pretty goddamn sure he forgot me. The whistle's, rolling eye's and snickers from all the passing guards we encountered was a pretty good indicator.

He would never fess up to it, but my big ass grin let him know that I knew.

…"Good afternoon Warden"
"Mister Frieze, right? Oh yah… how could forget, the guy that likes a close shave"

He started in with his hearty laugh as he scrounged around in his desk drawer looking for something.

He picked up a thick envelope and handed it to me…

"I need to be present when you open this… it's from the government"

He looked to be trying to refrain from coughing out another chuckle.

I started reading the cover letter, then glanced at the second page that had some columns of figures…

"You've got to be kidding me"

I read a little more…

"Get the hell outta here… they must be kidding"
"What is it Frieze?"

"The IRS is saying that I owe tax on the money I got in the robberies… it's considered Personal Income. Because I haven't reported it as such and haven't filed in six years there are substantial penalties. I need to report to the nearest IRS office and submit a check in the amount $428,170.08"

"They're not kidding. That's a pretty high figure, you must of gotten away with a lot of money. However, that is the law. I mean, it is a personal income in the sense of the words, isn't it?"

"It's not the original amount, that's way more than I took… like four times as much. The penalties alone are way more than I got. You know Warden, this sounds pretty serious, it may be best if I report to them right away. Could I borrow your car?"

"Frieze, every time I see you it turns out to be something comical, I have actually brought up your escapades in dinner conversations, for some reason you're always an enjoyable encounter. Listen, if you need assistance to send a response let your Command Center know to inform me"

"Thanks Warden… and about your car?"

"Get the hell outa here. Oh, wait a minute. Hold on, what's this I hear about some deal that happened early this morning, you and a can of chocolate pudding or something. Lt. said he's going to make some copies of a photo this afternoon and I won't believe it"

"The photo will be self-explanatory… if there isn't anything else, may I get back to Unit A"

"Officer Slacker, would you take Inmate Frieze back to his housing unit"

God damn Lt. is really milking my puddingfest.

Man that was tasty.

I didn't like losing ANY good time but if someone offered me another #10 can of Chocolate Pudding for an extra day in here it would be one tough-ass decision.

I threw the letter on my bunk and headed for the shower.

"Hey Scotty... Pi-nuc tourney tonight... you in?"
"Absofreakamente hombre"

I hadn't played any Pi-nuc for a long time... between my work on SSIIJ6Y, Spanish lessons and vacationing at my favorite All Inclusive Resort, I lost contact with the under the radar boys.

It was time to have a night of relax.

The day room was packed... card games, chess, dominos and of course the three TV's.. Mexican, Movies, Sports. I had never seen the room with so much activity. I couldn't help but think about the last time I had been in here... I looked over to a spot about twenty feet from my cell door... that was the epitome of hilarious.

"Scotty, get over here... I don't know why you got that big ass smile go'n on, I'm gonna whup yo ass son... where's your stamps, throw 'em in the pile"

Bart's got a lot of energy, good dude... the judge gave him thirty five years for the same crime that I committed. I felt bad for him. I was almost embarrassed when I told him my sentence. He did his robberies in Iowa, the difference being that he and a couple of other guys brandished their weapons.

Still thirty five years is a pretty healthy chunk of a man's life.

They didn't get caught in the bank or by good police work. One of the most amazing stat's about the dudes in here, most are in here because their girlfriend, wife etc. ratted on them.

I'm telling you it was like EVERYONE you talked to... that was the reason they got caught.

The girlfriend gets pissed off, finds a new boyfriend, catches the guy screwing around, he forgot to take the trash out… whatever. She goes in, grabs most of the drugs for a girlfriend to hold, then drops a dime…

"Yes, hello Mr. Police Department, I just found out that my husband is selling drugs out of our house. I wanted to report this because I am against the use of drugs, even though I've been convicted three times for possession… I can even show you where all the drugs are right now. Oh… and I also just found out that his good friend… she looks at the name the girlfriend wrote down, the guy she wanted to rat on, before she hauled ass with the drugs… Ah yes... his good friend ------------ is selling drugs also"

I'd prefer that GODZILLA was pissed off at me, instead of a chick.

A woman scorned… I don't even know how that phrase ends, don't need to, don't want to. I just <u>hear</u> those three words and chills go down my spine.

Scotty's "Tip for the Day Life"… Don't tell 'em jack.

LORAINE BOBBIT

Seven of the under the radar boys were there and some new dude. We all got our soda, coffee, pisto and the shuffling started…

 "Hey Fitz… where's Ronnie?"
"You know what man, he's been act'n pretty strange lately bro, I don't know what's go'n on with him, you know… like when you say something to him he acts like he's pissed off at you or something"

"Somebody should pull him up and ask him, maybe he's got problems we can help him out with. Ah man, I like Ronnie, he keeps to himself. Fitz... you and me, we're going to talk to him tomorrow, all right?"
"Yah... you got it. Right now, Scotty my man, I'm go'n to relieve you of your Postal Communication Ability. Pay attention, I don't want you cry'n tomorrow saying you had shit on your mind"

I did have Ronnie on my mind for a moment, a car thief... turned burglar, turned home invader, turned commercial business invader, turned stocks & bond thief, turned prisoner #441617167. His older brothers got him started. His stature being like that of a horse jockey... he was thief perfect. He told me that he could climb into a Gnat's ass wearing a sombrero while carrying his toolbox.

We got down to some serious card play'n.

The pod was holding the crowd late, I had been looking at the clock as it approached 9:45, normally the guards were mixing in the crowd dropping the hint... close to lock-down start wrapping up your games. 9:55 and nobody's moving. What's up?

What did they do... change the rules while I was eating my pudding. What the hell... it's 10:05 and nobody's moving.

"Fitz, what's up with lock-down... look at the clock bro"
"If you could read you would have known that a new give ém something because tomorrow we need to take something schedule for holiday hours came out. Didn't you notice that a lot of dudes didn't work today?"
"No I didn't. I was tied up in business meetings all day... you know, the Doc, Lt., the Warden, they just can't make a decision without my counsel"
"I thought maybe you were tied up with another photo-op"
"Ah shit, you heard about that, man I wanted to keep that out of the press"

"You know Willy, Lt's clerk? Your photo somehow got mixed up with some other papers he needed to copy. It's just a shitty black & white, it looks like a photo of a black dude with white rings around his eyes, but If you look at it real good... you pop out"

"Damn it. So what's the freakin holiday"

"Labor day man... That's funny, keep it out of the press. You didn't see the one somebody taped to your cell door. Fuck Scotty, the cactus are snicker'n when you pass by ém. Tell me bro, was that pudding good"

"Off the Charts"

Every once and a while Ronnie would walk out to the railing just outside of his cell and stand there, coffee cup in hand, viewing the action down below. His house was on the upper tier, so he could take in the whole panorama. He seemed to be focused on the group of tables that were controlled by some questionable citizens of our unfair town.

I was worried about him.

At about 11:30 I looked up to see Ronnie out of his cell again, drinking coffee and looking pre-occupied.

"Let's go Scotty, your play... damn dude, pay attention"

"Hey man, I'm worried about Ronnie, he's just standing up there drinking coffee"

The three all looked up as I made my play.

"You better check on those peepers of yours... you be seeing ghosts my man"

I looked back up at an empty railing. The crowd was starting to thin and I was happy with that... way past my bedtime.

I could see the table clearly now that seemed to have captured Ronnie's attention. Just as I thought, filled with the assholes.

It's clear to me... somebody's fucking with him.

Now that I think about it, the asshole with his back to me... a rather large fellow, has been hanging out on the upper tier lately. The other day, there was a bit of a ruckus up there that got squelched fast, but I'm pretty sure he was the instigator.

As I had been looking at the table I saw Ronnie appear, he was walking towards the micro-wave, I guess to heat up his coffee.

I made my play, collected the book I won and glanced back at the Micro-wave as it dinged. Ronnie opened the door and glanced over his shoulder in the direction of the prick table before he removed his coffee.

Uh oh... something's up, Scotty's antenna picked up some serious freak'n interference.

What the fuck is he up to???

"Hey Fitz... Shit's about to go down, dude... come on, let's go get Ronnie"

I saw Ronnie grab his cup, flip a quick U and head straight for the Prick table.

"FITZ!!"

As I stood up, Ronnie came up to the back of Instigator dude and poured his coffee on the top of his head.

I have NEVER heard a man scream like that before... nor after.

It was blood curdling.

All the guys at the table and around it spread backwards, some… actually flying backwards out of their chairs, landing on their backs.

All hell broke loose… Instigator was running around the table holding the sides of his head… SCREAMING.

The sirens went off, guards ran in armed for war.

I looked at Ronnie, who was frozen about ten feet from where Instigator landed on the floor.

Ronnie stepped back and threw the coffee cup at Instigator's head, where he laid silent on the floor…

"FUCK YOU, I AIN'T NO CHICK, YOU ARE!!" "FUCK YOU MOTHER FUCKER, YOU'RE THE BITCH"   "FUCK YOU" "LOOK AT YOU NOW"

Those words meant one thing… ABUSE.

Ronnie kept repeating this mantra as the guards jammed him into the wall, he was audibly crying as the tears poured down his face. There was nothing I could do but watch.

There must have been fifty guards in the pod by now.

After everyone had been pushed into their cells the sirens were turned off.

Ronnie was on the floor with two guards keeping him immobile with their knees on his neck and legs. I could just catch the scene if I put my cheek on the side of the viewing pane.

There was a large puddle of fluids spreading from the head of the silent Instigator dude. I could see that his face or what used to be his face, was gone.

Before they placed a sheet over him I noticed that his eye sockets were nothing but black holes, everything that used to have flesh above his shoulders was now making up the contents in the puddle.

Four guards surrounded Ronnie and hoisted him off the floor.

As they started to lead him away I got down on my knees and placed my face on the floor at the bottom of the cell door…

"RONNIE, YOU'RE THE MAN, NEVER A DOUBT BRO, YOU'RE THE BIGGEST MAN I EVER MET"

I stayed where I was at until about three, just sitting there with my back against the wall, knees up with my head in my hands.

My body shook for a hour or so… I was in shock.

All I could think about is how many guys here are being subjected to the abuse Ronnie had just put an end to.

There is a whole bunch of evil here. Instigator dude got what was coming to him. The one thing that bothers me most about this tragedy is that Instigator, doing a life gig, just got a free pass to exit.

The exit was just sealed for Ronnie.

The entire prison was in lock-down for the next three days.

The convicts that qualified to be Trustees, low level custody convicts, worked as clerks in the various offices responsible for the functioning of the facility.

The facts were leaked within 6 hours.

Soon the network spread the news... lunch came to the slot in cell doors consisting of a food tray and a whisper.

There were about three believable versions, not until the fourth day after the incident did I learn the truth.

I made an appointment with Doc to check my hand that had been injured when Senor too long a name's ear ran into my fist.

Out of the blue the pain just flared up...

"I really need to see the Doc"

When I walked into Doc's office he stood up and started to grab my arm to look at my hand, I pulled it away...

"Doc... I'm here about Ronnie"

It turns out that Ronnie had a brother doing time in Soledad and he got himself into a jam with debts... drug debts. Ronnie had to help pay it off or his brother was going to lose his head. Ronnie was making it good by paying with his weekly store. He took it a step further and started abusing Ronnie on the threat of his brother's life.

When Instigator took it to a level that was sexually unnatural for Ronnie, he fixed the problem.

Señor Instigator was DOA by the time he arrived to the hospital, in fact he ceased to exist when he hit the floor.

Seems that Ronnie put hair conditioner in his coffee cup and when his napalm solution got to boiling nicely he poured it on the head of Instigator.

If boiling coffee or water had been used, the solution would immediately start cooling to the core temperature of the surface it was poured upon contact. It would have caused damage and pain, but death would have been unlikely.

The properties in the ingredients used for hair conditioner however, hold the temperature much longer, cooling is a very slow process.

The best example Doc gave me in describing the solution that Ronnie concocted was napalm, molten lava.

Ronnie was transferred to San Antonio for Psychiatric evaluation and will be charged with first degree murder upon discharge.

Personally, I think he should be nominated for the Medal of Valor. God bless you Ronnie.

In the following week all the uproar over Instigator losing face in front of everyone had subsided.
(I had to write it, enjoyed writing it. Irreverence was intended)

There were plenty of daily abuse victims, fights, scams, drug overdoses and what not, to keep everyone's mind occupied and not dwelling on the Labor day incident.

I however, dwelled.

I felt like if I had been a little more perceptive earlier in the night, I could have helped Ronnie.

Fitz said the only Fix for Ronnie was what took place.

I had walked out into the dayroom to heat up my coffee, they were doing some construction over by the chow hall, so I didn't have to clean windows.

While I waited for the ding I watched the happenings of the day on the TV that had a news program going. That was different, normally it always had cartoons on that TV.

I grabbed my cup and just as I was passing by a Jet flew right into a skyscraper. I backed up and looked again, there were a couple of guys in front of the set...

"Is that a movie preview or did that really just happen?"
"I think that just happened in New York"
"You're shit'n me... really?"

I sat down at the table and sure enough... a jet just flew into one of the Twin Towers in New York City. As we watched another plane came into view, it looked like it was turning to line up with the buildings.

"God damn, that plane is going to hit the building too"

As it slammed into the other building the guards came out of the Command Center and pretty soon the dayroom had all three TV's showing the scene.

"It looked like they did that on purpose!!"

Soon there was debate and conjecture between convicts and convicts, convicts with guards, counselors with guards. it was almost like listening to people discussing something with a little compassion, true concern and yes... intelligence.

About thirty minutes after the second plane hit the tower the emergency sirens started going off.

The Prison was now under full emergency lock-down.

Every cell viewing pane had a face in it trying to see the TV's.

The prison was under a "Code Red" lock-down for three weeks, apparently the United States Government was concerned that additional strikes may take place on American soil. Should a war break out in the USA, they didn't want dangerous criminals breaking free and running amuck in the streets.

A rumor started circulating through the Food Cart News & What Else Do You Need Agency, that should a war break out on American soil, there is a mandate that instructs the Federal Correctional Institutions to euthanize all prisoners currently housed in Maximum Custody Units.

I didn't know if this is truly a mandate or not, still don't... I am sure that if it were true, it wouldn't be readily available information for the common folk.

I spent my three weeks trying to figure a plan on my action, should this be correct information.

This was the time,
during which I was doing my time,
that had me most concerned that it was my time.

I found myself in the most enviable position, six months short. This is where it is critical that you are in constant vigilance of your surroundings.

The asshole convicts, sharks... all the Type A's, have you in their sights. For the life of me I don't understand the reasoning or satisfaction factor.

They don't want you to get released.

Their mission is to get you to violate some rule so there will be more time tacked on to your sentence. Frank had mentioned this to me before he was released, but I didn't get to see it firsthand. He had arranged to be re-located into the Low Level Custody building six months prior to his release.

Clerks privileges.

A fellow named Nugget had just made it through the asshole nets and gauntlets. He was to be released in the morning, after doing thirty three calendars.

At the smokers patio the night before I could hear the conversation he was having with a couple of guys...

"Don't let Billy throw anythin out, he don't believe me. I'm tell'n ya... I'll see ya fur late chow"

Now, I'm not a rubber necker and where I'm at is definitely a place you don't want to be one. However, I was one very curious dude as to the meaning of his comment.

The siren went off ending the conversation.

I knew Nugget only in passing... he was in a different unit.

I couldn't ask anyone because that would confirm rubber neck status and that would be a serious violation of the Convict Code. I think I saw it in Addendum Three, Sub-section 3A-72D under the heading; "Who in the fuck invited you into this conversation"

I was left in the dark... a closet RN.

The previous night's conversation was out of mind as I was catching the day's last chance to smoke.

... "Nugget you old dog, welcome home"

I flipped around to catch Nugget strolling up, sport'n his brilliant four and a half tooth chew tone smile...

"I told you boy's, Nugget don't lie. I did everthin' I said I'd do. It sure is scary out there, it's nice to be back home"

Damn that siren.

Just as I entered the Unit there were two convicts standing outside the laundry facilities talking, as I passed I heard Nuggets name.

I slammed on the ABS and dropped to re-tie the laces on my orange Detention Issue slip-on Vans.

These guys were clown'n Nugget pretty good...

"That fuck'n Nugget, he had a large Pizza and drank two pitchers of beer. Then he robbed a Security Pacific with a note... he grabbed his big take of $217.00, went out and just sat on the curb wait'n for the cops to show up so they could give him a ride back here"

I figured my laces were tight enough and that I had heard enough.

Fitz was in the cell when I entered, he wouldn't call me on coming out of the closet...

"Did you hear about what that Nugget idiot did?"
"Yah... it happens all the time. A lot of these guys don't have anything out there, they've spent most of their life in Prison. This is home, the only friends they have are in here... they're Institutionalized"
"Sad"
"If you saw him tonight, would you say he looked sad to you?"
"Not really"
"Electricity, water, food, hot showers... CABLE. The system works"

With a tense three months left, the Under the Radar Boys and I had a New Year's celebration in my cell.

Fitz, with eleven years left on his sentence, took Franks spot when he left. He will then be in control of House 109 when I'm released, allowing himself the opportunity to select the person he wants as a Celly...

and the horses go round and round.

The boy's got together, pitched in their books of stamps and bought two bags of Pisto, homemade wine/moonshine.

Just a little yeast, a lot of sugar and any and every piece of fruit you can get your hands on go into a trash bag. Fill with a couple of gallons of water; find a hiding spot up in the ceiling, vents, Rec room… wherever the guards last searched.

They know all the hiding spots.

If you watch them close enough, patterns develop in the manner in which their search is conducted.

If Pattern Watcher dude is doing his job well, Pisto Maker dude knows where the best stash spots are with the least likely hood of discovery.

The In Charge of Paying off the Guards dude is also a key factor in the assurance of a fine year's harvest.

I've had periods in my life that I have consumed more alcohol than I should have, but generally I'm not a big drinker.

When I was in my early thirties I viewed a video from a party I had been at… Scotty was an absolute fool, a buffoon. The Life of the Party that woke up the next morning thinking that the previous night's party was the best time he had ever had.

I was the complete asshole everyone was trying to avoid.

The video was showing people rolling their eyes when I left their sides, making excuses to leave when I tried to join in on the conversation. Unquestionably one of the most embarrassing and the most enlightening moments in my life.

Since, I have ceased imbibing to the extreme.

New Years 2003 was an exception.

The morning of January 2nd will go into the Scotty's book of Personal World Records under brutal hangovers. I wanted to die, prayed for the euthanasia gases to spew into the cell.

It lasted for three days.

There has not been any entry in the book under that category since. Truth be known... there are no other entries in the book in ANY category.

The UTRB surrounded me in a protective cocoon, whenever a public appearance was required, fading any heat even remotely headed in my direction.

There were a few attempts, not worthy of print.

They took it as a personal victory against evil and were as proud as the parents of the recipient at a Valedictorian Ceremony.

Scotty was six hours short.

The night before my release I unceremoniously made out my will, this is very important to get correct.

OK, who needed or wanted my speakers?

Bart got my two tide box speakers that I had made from 8 transistor radio speakers.

Bobby got my fairly new Nikes, his 11" hooves were the closest to my 13's.

Fitz got all the micro-ware.

My good friend Jungle Jimmy had size fifteens so mine would have been a little snug… fortunately he didn't need new planks. I wanted to leave him something important so he'd remember me, so all my educational materials and my MOST cherished and quite substantial collection of sample illustrations depicting how women can be art also, went down under his name. I hope he's alright with that, there aren't that many articles.

When I had finished it was one in the morning.

I'll be damned, Backstroke was working and his face popped up in the viewing pane at 4:05am, just as the cell door clicked.

My one last chance to fuck with him… blown opportunity.

DAAAAAMN, I wish I would have known he was working.

"You ready Frieze?"
"Have been for about six years, four months, two weeks and six days"
"By the way Frieze, I just gotta tell ya, that WAS a good one"

My last memory of that shit hole was hearing the sentiments coming from under the cell doors of some pretty fair blokes as I walked through the day room…

"Good luck bro, don't ever want to see you again"
"Love ya Scotty, good luck"
"You da man Scottster"
"Remember to eat at Greasy Tony's for me"
"Fuck Greasy Tony's, eat a beautiful blond for me"

GOD BLESS YOU BOYS… I won't ever forget ya.

Freedom... kind of

Part of the release process was spending mandatory time at the Observation House, which was basically a baby prison complex on the outskirts of Tucson, you were also required to attend re-introduction into society classes.

I had one more obligation before I could actually move about, with prior written permission of course.

My appointment to meet the Parole Officer assigned to be my Supervisor was set for 8 am the following day. I had been duly informed that this person had complete authority over me and with just a stroke of their pen I would be back in Prison for 5-10 years, depending on the violation, without recourse.

I never thought a ride on a bus would be such a momentous occasion however, with the exception of the taxi ride from the Prison gates to the Observation house, this was the first time I had been on the streets in eight years, as a free man.

When you are caught up in daily life you don't notice the changes taking place around you, when you are removed from life for a period of eight years and then suddenly reappear, the changes... progression, are apparent.

So, to say that I was like a wide eyed kid in a candy store would be an understatement.

"Federal Court Buildings... next stop"

Stepping into the main complex gave me the "Well, you're not exactly free yet" feeling once I arrived at the metal detector and had been asked to empty my pockets and remove my shoes.

Upon entering the Probation Department offices I was asked for my Prison Issued identification and told to take a seat.

The wall clock showed 7:50.

A large, overweight, un-kept man in uniform stepped through the front doors and said "Good Morning" to the uniformed gal in the screened, well fortified reception cage as he passed and quickly disappeared into the recesses.

Thinking this may be my Parole officer I glanced at the clock 9:10.

At 11:15 the reception officer told me to step through the door marked "Enter Only with Permission", go to the end of the hallway where I will find the office of Patricia Peterson, my Parole Officer.

Well, so much for my guess about Officer Un-kept. The door was open so I couldn't see a name plate, however I could see Officer Un-kept hunched over some files...

"I'm sorry, but I was told I would find Patricia Peterson' office here..."

Before I could say more Officer Un-kept looked up and barked...

"You did, I'm OFFICER Peterson... take a seat"

As He/She/It continued thumbing through the files I was trying to determine if this was a Boy named Sue kind of thing or what.

Well, let's see…. Short haircut, Brill-Creme comb-back complete with fenders, man shirt, man pants, man watch, man shoes, big barrel chest…

Whoa….wait a minute, that's not a barrel chest, that's pushed down boobs.

A wannabe a Dude chick.

Her and Alfredo need to swap recipes. How in the hell did she get that Peach fuzz mustache and those chin whiskers.

Ah, the wonders of steroids.

That's ok… to each his or her own. She's my PO, not my date.

However, I did just leave a place that had about 1200 guys that wouldn't have a problem overlooking her facial hair.

"Alright… as I said, I am OFFICER Peterson. You need to find a place to rent and a job, ASAP. Your days of Federal Sponsorship are up. While you stay at the "House" we will charge you $40 per day, starting tomorrow. Here are your Rules & Reg's. READ um and KNOW um, I don't accept excuses. Now, go through that door and pee in a cup, be back tomorrow, 8 am"

I did not say one single word… NOT ONE

As I exited the building I glanced at the unedited version of War and Peace I was handed. On the title page, in bold print, it read,

INTENSE PROBATION GUIDELINES
RULES and REGULATIONS

The Christopher Hyman provision.

How bad can this be?

I had a Pass until the 5pm "Count" at the House. There should be enough time to take care of personal matters such as buying all those items that had been provided to me for the past eight years by the United States Government…. including underwear.

The luxury of being able to go into any chosen store and poke around at your leisure, looking at various items to purchase, is truly a gift from having freedom, not appreciated until taken away.

The next morning I stepped into the Federal Probation Office at 7:45 am, intent on following the mandates to the letter and determined to leap back into society with the proper mental attitude. I'm going to work my ass off and put this eight years behind me.

At 9:05 Officer Peterson entered and just as the day before, said good morning" to the receptionist, however, this time she glanced in my direction and without acknowledgement continued through to the back.

Various Parolees came into the reception area, registered, then were systematically called within ten to twenty minutes.

"Mr. Frieze, please enter and go to the end of the hallway, Officer Peterson is waiting for you"

I glanced at the clock… 11:30. Now, I have always been a punctual person, but hey this isn't my Ballgame so I'll just grin & bear it.

"SIT. Have you found a place to live or a job?"

"No, I am just starting to look"

"I didn't have time yesterday, but….."

"LISTEN… excuses are like ASSHOLES, look at my desk, I have stacks of em. Just give me the word and I can give you plenty more TIME, you now owe ME $40 rent."

I guess she owns the Observation House.

"Have you read the Guidelines?"

"Not completely"…

I wasn't about to say that I didn't have time.

"Well read it… I want it back tomorrow, with each page signed. I also want a list of places you looked at to rent and also the places you applied for work, now go through that door and pee in a cup, be back here tomorrow… 8 AM"

I wanted to say… "Will you be here?"

Easy Scott, this person has control of your fate.

On my way out of the building a fellow Parolee joined me on the walk to the bus stop.

His appointment had been at 11 am.

… "Hey, how's it going bro? They sure are brutal in there"

"What are you talking about… Es pinche nada. You check in once a week, tell them life is good and pee in a cup. Then you say, see you next week. My wife even pee's in a baggie for me and I keep it under my arm… you know, to keep it warm. Man, I sure hope she doesn't get pregnant… that'll be a bitch to explain"

"So who is your PO?"

"Hernandez… they're all the same"

Clearly you haven't met OFFICER Peterson.

On my way to a rental agency I thought... Maybe she's just testing me, this is just the initiation, to see if you're a volatile kind of person or not. That's alright, I can keep my cool.

By the time I arrived at the Rental Agency it was 1:30 and after explaining where I had been living for the past eight years, that I didn't have a job yet, however, I WILL pay my rent on time. Needless to say, the interest level of the agent dropped to below 0 on the Potential Client Meter.

I was summarily dismissed... with polite caution, of course.

Now, close to 3 pm, all I could think of was the list I had been told to have prepared of the places I looked at to rent and the job interviews I went on. I've got just under two hours, minus the bus ride back to the $40 a night mansion.

OK... Job first, I got off the bus at the Auto Mall, my place of employment for over six years... BEFORE.

Although I wasn't dressed with the mandatory Shirt & Tie interview apparel, I thought I would walk the two block "Every Make.. Every Model Mall" time to formulate a plan for tomorrow.

No sooner did I hit the sidewalk by the first dealership...

"Hey!! Frieze, is that you???"
"God-damn... when did you get out?"
"Hey... YOU GUYS... LOOK... it's Scotty"
"You gotta come in, nobody's gonna believe this, when did you get out?"
"HEY..EVERYBODY..... IT'S SCOTTY FRIEZE!!!!!!"
"Hey Trevor, DUDE... cool it. STOP!!! I don't want to see anyone right now, come on bro, give me a break"

I forgot… Sales guys scan the perimeter like Hawks seeking Prey.

Trevor, a solid guy and a great salesman was one of the best.

The fact that he was a single parent raising two kids, ages four & six, made him a Saint in my book.
A good friend, I respected him a lot.

"Hey Trev, listen… I just got out and I want to fly below the radar if you know what I mean, so enough with the announcement. I'll be back tomorrow, maybe looking for work. Would you put out some feelers for me, you know.. see if that's even a possibility. I sure would appreciate it. Hey man, it's really good to see you again, I'm guess'n you own this place by now"

He gave me that 20+ cars a month smile…

"Why would I want to, I make more money sell'n and go'n home with zero stress"
"I'll be by around two tomorrow, by the way, how are the kids?"
"Katie just started High School, they'll be excited to see you"
"Can't wait, it's fucking great to see you again bro"

I walked about ten feet, then turned back…

"Hey Trev, I sure hope Katie grew in those two front teeth since I've seen her last, if not she's going to have a tough time in High School"
"I'll tell her you said that"
"One more thing… do me a favor and keep an eye out for me, I really don't feel like going in to look for you… thanks"

I forgot that Trevor can't keep an eye out for me, he'd be blind, he lost an eye while playing football. It was a freak accident but he is pretty good natured about it, sometimes even clowning himself.

You sure couldn't tell, the prosthesis was remarkable.

I decided to turn around and go back to the bus stop, seeing Trevor was better than ten personal interviews, he'd let me know what's up.

Feeling GREAT about running into my old friend Trevor Barrington, I suddenly caught myself grinning broadly.

I got back to the House about 4:15 and sitting outside the Quonset hut were a group of my fellow detainees discussing the day's events. Not being one to sit around and shoot the shit with the boys, I sat to the side having a smoke, listening to their recounting of the day's events. All were in the same situation as I was. Fresh out of prison and meeting their PO's for the first time. I was surprised that they were all taking it in stride, no real complaints, other than having to go in one day a week to report and pee.

"Hey man… it's no big deal; I can handle thirty minutes a week"

The main complaint seemed to be that they were all assigned a color, every morning they would have to call in and if they had the "Color of the day" it was an extra pee deposit day.

One guy was saying….

"Hey don't sweat it, my brother's been on Parole for over a year and he said most of the time they're too busy so you get recording saying… No color today, what's funny is if you have to go in any way that day, they're just all sittin' around doin' nothin'. They don't want to see us… we don't want to see them"

One day a week?!??!?

I've had to go in three out of four days, 4 hours a crack… what the hell is going on with my PO.

I just had to ask...

"Are any of you on Intense Probation?"

The guy with all the answers said...

"Ah, that ain't nothin', you just have to go in two days a week, instead of one"

OK... maybe she's just testing me. She'll probably tell me about the two mandatory days today.

Again, no one was impressed with my punctuality, however I felt like I was gaining ground when I was called to the office by 10:30.

"Sit... I told you to bring the Guideline back with your signature, set it on my desk. I also told you to bring me a list of rentals and job interviews you've been on. Show me the list, then TELL me where you have been"
"Look, I haven't..."
"LOOOOK!!... You WILL address me by OFFICER PETERSON. Are you showing me an attitude? Don't EVER say LOOK to me in that manner again or you'll be on the next bus back to where you belong. Do you understand me? I was warned about you"

Warned about me... By who? WTF...

"Officer Peterson, I have been in this office 4 of the 9 hours I am allowed out each day, I am still trying to get things together, I think I will be able to secure a job by the end of the week"
"Think and hopefully aren't gonna fly, you now owe me $80 for your lodging and you don't have a job, this department doesn't extend credit for very long. You better have some answers, not excuses for me tomorrow morning... 8 am. Pee and get out of here"

All I could think of was… someone warned her about me. What in the hell is she talking about? I had a pretty good prison record… mas o menos, no enemies that I could think of.

Except……… CHRISTOPHER HYMAN!!

Nah, that was eight years ago, you're reading too much into this.

She'll mellow out once I get a job and a place to stay.

It was before noon and I'm off and running.

No matter what, I'm going to secure a job before five.

Trevor was out Hawk'n the lot when I rounded the corner and when he saw me he got that 20+ smile. I hoped he had some good news.

"Hey Frieze… I talked to Gary Patton, you remember Gary, don't you?"
"Yah sure… the Used Car Manager"
"Scotty, get with it bro, those are called Pre-owned vehicles now…
anyway, Gary's the GM now, you and he have always had a good relationship so he said he'd like to talk to you, he also asked if I would break the ice"…
"He can't offer you a position like you had, you know the insurance company requires Bonding of all Managers, but he'd like to have you on the floor…selling"
"Trev, that's the best news I've heard in eight years… where's Gary's office?"
"Hey Frieze…"

I looked back to see Trevor with that God-damn smile….

"You're not going to ROB us are you?… they haven't paid me my commissions this week."

When I walked out of Gary's office I must have been three feet off the ground, never happier to get a job in my life. All I could think of was delivering this news to OFFICER Peterson, maybe she'll lighten up on me.

Having spent about two hours with Gary catching up on all the happenings in the last eight years, from both sides, the news would have to wait until tomorrow and I start the day after.

I'm Back!!

I was called into the office at 9:30. Either Officer Peterson was anxious to belittle someone or she wanted to get out early. Or... it was Friday, maybe it was He/She/It Night at The Goat's Ass bar.

"I'm real busy today so... have you found a job?"
"Yes"
"YES??? You DID? Where?

After telling her the good news about having an old employer hire me and that I could start tomorrow she informed me that I can't accept a job until SHE approves it...

"You are already breaking the rules and that's a serious violation. I want you to re-read the Regulations this weekend, because I will not accept another violation. I am going to overlook this infraction and allow you to begin tomorrow because you are already behind $200 for your housing. Subject, of course, to MY final approval, after I interview your new employer"

My good news seemed to fall a little short, actually disappointing to her... NOT the reception I had hoped for.

"Write down all the information on the Employment Verification form, then go pee. Be back here 8 am on Monday"

"I am supposed to be at work on Monday at 8 am"

"There you go. You're already messing with system. Well, my bad. I was warned, until when?"

"The shifts are 8 am-3 pm/3 pm-10 pm. I thought I would work both shifts to try to get caught-up"

"You thought wrong, so don't think, be here at three fifteen."

"Can I at least come in at three thirty, it's about a twenty minute bus ride. I would hate to have to ask my boss if I could leave early, you know... new job and all"

"THREE FIFTEEN... not a second later or I'll consider you in violation"

Man... this is going to be a tough five years if this is any indication of what's to come. As I left I was pre-occupied with what she had said... "WARNED"

This god damn "I've been warned" crap is starting to wear a little thin. Ah well, this isn't going to ruin what I have been anxiously awaiting for... an afternoon with two beautiful women.
OOOOH YAAAAH!!!

I've got a four hour Pass, which is probably not going to be enough time, if you know I mean.

It has been quite a few years for Christ sake.

I also needed to do some personal shopping.

I had to submit a form explaining where I would be meeting them for lunch and what we would be doing afterwards. We had arranged to meet at a local Mexican restaurant, so I headed off towards the bus stop.

It was time to spend some waaay overdue privacy with the two most gorgeous women I could think of.

That's right... TWO.

When I stepped into the restaurant it took my eyes a moment to adjust from the brightness outside and then I saw them.

My daughter's smiles made me feel like my entire life was worth this single moment. Did I really play a part in creating these two wonderful human beings?

After tearful hugs, that would have been fine with me to continue for the rest of my life, we sat and it seemed as if the eight years that had separated us just melted away.

They looked like their Mom, had a sweet style to their speech, with mannerisms that took me back twenty years.

That was wonderful, I couldn't dream of a better role model.

Good job, Janie.

They wanted to hear about my last eight years, which I really wasn't ready to get into and I wanted to hear about their last eight.

I won.

So much had transpired... they both graduated from U of A and both had married two handsome, well adjusted lads they had met in college. I had met the two of them on one of the Christmas visits that I felt confident that the guards wouldn't insist on conducting extensive searches of visitors.

The girls chose two good guys, a fathers nightmare dispersed.

I suddenly realized that with all the catching up the time had flown by and I had only one and a half hours to get back to the House

I still needed to purchase Car sellin' duds... Shirts, ties, slacks, etc...

Dana & Lory insisted on driving me... during which they expressed my need for their assistance with the proper selections.

I have to admit, I am the typical guy that hates to shop. I go in, grab it, pay for it and get the hell out... as fast as possible. This time however, goes down in my book as the most enjoyable shopping experience of my life. Rif & Lors, don't ask me how they got their nicknames, held items up against me, switching & matching, debating the garments worthiness.

I felt like a king and didn't want it to ever end.

The girls dropped me off at the "House", with promises to not let much time slip by before we do this again.

I grabbed my bags and returned to reality.

It was close to midnight by the time I had washed, ironed and shined all that was necessary to present myself well on my first day at work... IN OVER 8 YEARS!!!!

The bus stopped at the corner of the mall and as I exited there was a swarm of butterflies inside my body that left me a bit barren in the confidence cabinet.

Yes, I was nervous, I haven't even been in a car for 8 years.

How much has changed??

There were even a couple of models I hadn't even heard of.

Scott, shake it off, you've had bigger obstacles… HANDLE IT.

I threw my shoulders back, did a little shake of my body to rid myself of these insecurity pests and walked up the driveway.

Big memories when I entered the front doors of Precision Chevrolet… my old/new place of employment.

The first person I see as I enter is Trevor, coffee in hand and busy reviewing the inventory print out.

Let me tell you, a friend for many years, I have always been impressed with this dude. He gets up at 4 am, prepares the bag lunches for his kids, presses everyone's clothes, makes sure everyone bathes, takes them to school at two different locations and is still the first one to work. Give me a freak'n break… IMPRESSIVE.

"Hey Scotty… you're early, they haven't opened the vault yet"
"God-damn it Trev.. I'm already nervous enough without you clown'n me"
"NERVOUS!! YOU? You've always been tops in Sales… well you know… right behind me at least."

There's that damn smile again.

"Dude, I need you to help me with inventory, new shit, you know… catch me up"
"Frieze, what the fuck, the customer always knows more about the car than we do, you leave your memory somewhere? The Internet… they're buying YOU… at least that was what you used to teach. Remember dick weed? I can only imagine what it's like to just be gone for eight years and try to pick up like it was the next day. Just be YOU and you'll be alright"

Man, I sure hope I can remember the Old Scotty.

Here comes that swarm again.

The front doors started swinging open every couple of minutes as the employees from various departments filed in.

Time for the morning Sales meeting.

Some things just don't change with the passage of time. The morning sales meeting at a large Automobile Dealership being one of those.

Long sleeve Shirts & Ties started filing in, cup of coffee in one hand, mandatory notebook in the other.

You could choose any notebook in that room and return it to the store from which it was purchased... for a full refund. Still as crisp, clean and blank as the day it was purchased.

I looked around seeing many familiar faces... some with nods of greeting, others with double takes of shock.

Not anything I wasn't expecting.

Gary called everyone's attention and began to announce the Sales from the previous day... each receiving applause and a little clown'n.

Of course, Trevor´s name was mentioned twice.

With fourteen minutes down of the normal fifteen minute meeting...

"We are joined this morning by a familiar face to many... a guy with a wealth of experience"

Ah Gary, don't do THIS to me... thought I made it.

... "So for you that don't know him, I would like to introduce Scott Frieze. Scotty, would you stand up and tell us a little about yourself"

Leaning over to Trevor I whispered....

"That God-damn Gary"

I stood up rapidly and after an extended pause suddenly barked "NO" and sat back down. I looked around to see big ass grins on the faces of the knowns, disappointment on the unknowns.

Hoots & laughter broke the silence.

With a pronounced smirk, Gary yelled... "MEETING AJOURNED!!!"

Trevor slapped me on the back...

"Thanks bro, I just won 30 bucks"

The lesson I learned from my first day in a Salesroom at an Automobile Dealership will be indelibly etched into my mind forever.

The embarrassment and frustration had been equally mixed to the nth degree. How anyone could bet Trevor that I would fall for it again is beyond me.

On the first day of a Green Pea´s introduction at the Sales meeting He or She is asked to "Please stand up and tell everyone a little bit about yourself" Of course, the needle on the Green Pea's anxiety meter starts tweak'n when asked without notice to deliver a quick autobiography. As soon as the first word comes out everyone in the room yells... "Sit down,   SIT DOWN!!! NOBODY CARES!!   SIT DOWN NOBODY CARES!!!"

This is such an unexpected occurrence their anxiety needle pins the far red and stays.

The GP is now standing there dumbfounded.

Once the chanting stops most individuals try to continue… only to be quieted by the chorus once more.

By this time most will take their seat in shock and embarrassment.

If the Manager is in the mood he will say…

"Hey knock it off;   this new guy/gal has an interesting background. Listen… I'm sorry about that… everyone PLEASE, Quiet Down everyone!!! Let's try that again. Please, stand up and tell us about yourself"

If you turn out to be one the poor bastards that do try again, an even louder chorus castigates you… "Sit down!!! SIT DOWN!!! NOBODY CARES!!!!

This time however, the embarrassment is tenfold. I know… once being one of those poor bastards.

When the meeting breaks everyone gives the Green Pea a slap on the back or a handshake helping the poor recipient recover.

Coffee cups in hand, Trevor and I walked the lot while I gave him the Short version of my past eight years. I also filled him in on my obligation to abide by very strict, Intensive Parole guidelines administered by a very strict Overly Intense Parole Officer.

… "Frieze, you just got out from being locked up for eight years, I'd think this would be a freak'n cake walk in comparison. I mean how bad can He/She/It be? Dude… YOU'RE FREE AGAIN!!!"

With a grand slap on my back he took off, spotting the first Up of the day. Even when in deep conversation Trev ALWAYS had his radar activated.

.

I headed for the showroom, where I planned on reviewing the Inventory print out, when I heard a voice…

"Are you a salesman?"

I did a three-sixty, nobody in sight.

"Are you a salesman sir?

I started thinking that a couple of the sales fools were mess'n with me but when I took a step forward, trying to follow the voice … sure enough, there was miniature "Up", in between a couple of 4x4's, about eye-level with the door handles.

"Good morning sir… yes, I'm a salesman here, how may I help you?"
"Well, if you could tell me a little about these trucks, you see my grandson just graduated High School, with Honors I might add. He needs something to get him to college"

What a perfect "Up" for me. I had a bit of the first day jitters.

Wow… It's been a long time. What a great old geez this guy turned out to be. We sat in my office… Ok, CUBICLE, going through the brochures and the Specs manual until he finally asked if I would give him a ride in it. After literally picking him up and putting him in the passenger seat we went for a ride up Oracle Road, northbound, to a spot that I remembered was a good place to test 4 wheel drive. Upon pulling off the road I explained that I would now show him the 4x4 power this particular vehicle possessed.

"Oh no!! I don't want you to get it dirty... No, No, please"
"It's alright Mr. Jenkins, I'm not going to hurt it at all, besides, I want to give the guys in the wash bay back at the Dealership a nice jolt of job security"

He didn't quite get my joke and insisted that we go directly back to the dealership. It was a return trip without conversation and I began thinking that maybe I had frightened him a bit.

He broke the silence...

"I hope it's ok that we didn't go in the dirt, it's just that I want it to be just like it is when my grandson gets it"

Now I realize that it has been a very long time since I've been on the Line selling cars... even well before my eight year vacation, however, I am pretty damn sure that his comment is way up at the top on the training list "Recognizing Client Buying Signs"... maybe number one, two and three.

Without further conversation we arrived back at the Dealership safe and dirt free.

... "Let's sit down and discuss how we will get this surprise to your grandson"

While writing down the information on the truck Mr. Jenkins kept himself busy looking through the various brochures on the table.

"Well Mr. Jenkins, is there anything you may want to add to the truck?"
"Add?... What do you mean by add?"
"There are a lot of accessories available. There is one I would like to suggest, that is if you ever plan on riding with your grandson. How about some steps below the doors for easier access"

"You can do that??"

If you ever could script how your first Up would be after a long layoff… Mr. Jenkins would be casted, hands down.

"Let's see… with Steps, the total comes to $43, 560.00"

Now… the rule in Sales is that you sit back and NOT say another word. Most salespeople feel that they now need to justify the figure… nope. If you think that you need to throw in some additional justification, you shouldn't be discussing the price yet.

Andy, my first Sales manager used to say Zip your Lip….

"It will cost money from the next person that opens his mouth"

I looked up from my Purchase Order form to see a price shocked white faced gentleman… all bug-eyed with his mouth hanging wide open…

"Wow!!... I didn't realize that these were so expensive"

Most customers go to the price sticker on the window first and then look at the vehicle.

I just now realized that he couldn't, it was three feet above his head. I forgot to do a "Price feeler" with him on the lot. OOOPS, a little rusty.

We sat there for a moment just looking at each other.

I was starting to get concerned that the blood would start spewing out of my mouth from biting my tongue.
Thanks Andy.

… "Well, if that is what it costs. I have been saving for this and I really want him to have it, I am so proud of him"

Another uncomfortable pause, the silence was almost a physical pain, my tongue may even require sutures after this one.

Keep it zipped. AHHH!!!!… The pain.

… "OK, I'll take it. Could you help me take it to my daughter's home to surprise him, of course I'll pay you for your time, I know this would take you away from your work."

Suddenly a big smile broke out on his face, followed by one on mine…. obviously for different reasons.

This is what salespeople dream about, it's called a "Lay Down", it rarely happens, but when it does it makes for a very nice paycheck.

I had him sign the Purchase Order form and headed over to the Desk Managers station to present the offer.

I stopped at an empty cubicle and wrote something on the bottom of the form.

When I arrived to "The Desk" it was Gary sitting there. Blake, the Manager had an errand to run.

"Well, well…. if it isn't the famous Scott Frieze. What took you so God damn long? A little outa step big stepper, eh? Whatcha got?"

Deskman are notorious for giving sales guys shit, it's part of the job, they like it and so does the sales guy, it's a stress reliever,

Gary was one of the best.

I handed him the Purchase Order, which he quickly perused and then said...

"What's this down here? He wants a $2,000 discount?? Did you tell him we don't discount 4x4's? What the fuck Frieze, did you go and get weak on me? Jeeeez... you want me to send in the Coffee Cart girl to bump him back up??"

I let Gary do his Schtick, which I knew he relished.

"You done Gary? Listen, that mild mannered gent in there is a shrewd dude, if we don't give him something he's walkin', I'm telling you a wolf in sheep's clothing. You go in there, he'll get more than two g's outa you"
"Listen Scotty... you know what you're doin' or at least you did. Go back in there and get me what you can. Right now we're sittin' on a 52 gross. Go... get out of here you weak stick. Jeeez... I'm really tempted to send the Coffee Chick in."

I was just happy as hell that I could still bluff Gary's ass off... he didn't take me up on going in himself... Hah!!

"Well, Mr. Jenkins, I've got good news... your Grandson is going to get his Dream Truck from you AND you happened to have selected a truck that had a $1,000 discount"
"Oh my God!!.... really?"
"Yes... Not only that, Precision Chevrolet would like to put those steps on as a gift to your grandson for Graduating, WITH Honors"

I went to inform Gary on the results of the heated negotiations and to get my drubbing. I couldn't be feeling better... first day, first sale. A nice gesture, for a nice gentleman.

I'm starting to feel like I am back in the mainstream again and it fells so damn good, a hint of the old Scotty.!!!!

... "$1,000!!! and the STAIRS!!! DAAAMN Frieze, I knew I should have sent in the Coffee Cart Chick, she would have at least gotten the money for the stairs. JEEEEZZUS KEEERIIST.... You do know that half the cost of the stairs comes out of your commission? Alright Scotty my man... that brings it down to an even $4.000 gross. See how he wants to pay"

Just as I reached the door...

"Hey Frieze... hard negotiator my ass, did you forget that I know you really well. This has all the markings of "Hey man, I liked the guy so I didn't want to Full Pop him. I remember your standard $2,000 to $1,000 drop. I guess the Joint didn't take the Softie out of you, nice work... welcome back. Now see if you remember how to deliver it properly and please don't give anything else away"

The standard commission is 50% of gross. I just made enough to get an apartment. I think it's time to call my brother Tim and my sister Joan for a little help with deposits and such.

My thinking may be a bit off kilter to some, but I have no problem looking at myself in the mirror after robbing a bank, however I would if I took advantage of an individual who put their trust in me or someone that just didn't know better. Can't do it... Never could.... Won't... and if that means I'm a Softie, so be it. It certainly makes shaving easier.

Late in the afternoon on Sunday I made another sale. Nothing like the good fortune of Mr. Jenkins, it was a Pre-owned vehicle that had few interested parties, so management was willing to Blow it Out. The $800 gross was just fine with me. Needing to meet with Officer Peterson early Monday morning and having a great beginning with my re-emergence into society I asked for Monday off to try to find a place to live.

I had spoken to all my family upon getting released and being a member of a very tight, loving and giving group of siblings everybody had made offers of assistance.

Well everybody… here comes the call.

At nine thirty I was summoned to He/She/Its office.

"Did you work this weekend?"

Never a …"Good morning" "Hello" "How is everything?" Always a bark of a command or demeaning statement. From what I have heard most of the Parolees seem to get along with their PO. Some have even said that they have given them a ride to help make an employment interview on time. How in the hell did I end up with this Person who seems to WANT me to fail, I thought a PO was supposed to help... at least a little

… "Yes. Two sales and I believe I made enough to rent a small place"
"Don't count your chickens. First you need to pay for the accommodations we are providing. I understand that the sum is up pretty high with you not making any attempts to pay it down"
"PAY IT DOWN???"
"Did YOU just raise your voice to me? I will NOT tolerate ANYONE raising their voice in MY office… you got that? You are sooo close to going back to where YOU belong"
"I didn't mean to raise my voice, I'm just a little shocked that you're this hard on me, I mean COME ON I just NOW got a job, give me a break, I'm doing everything possible to conform to your rules AND get my shit together as far as a home and whatnot"
"My job isn't to give you breaks, it seems to me that you already used up your breaks in life when Judge Goldstein ONLY gave you eight fucking years for YOUR crimes. Now I have a busy day, including having to interview your new employer, so get out."

I started to say something but thought better of it. I was feeling a bit shell shocked from the bombing I just took.

As I was standing up to leave...

"You better not forget to pee and you are to be here tomorrow at eight am. Do NOT be late, now get outta here"

You know... I've never hit a chick before, but GOD DAMN I want to knock her fuck out, wait patiently until she wakes up and then knock her fuck out again.

Upon exiting the building I felt the fresh morning air of Tucson on my face. What a wonderful feeling being free again, even with Officer He/She/It trying to make it miserable.

I filled my lungs with as deep of a breath possible and as I slowly let it go so went the previous 30 minutes of my life.

I'm free... well kind of and I've paid my debt to society, at least as much as Judge Goldstein had deemed appropriate. I am NOT going to give Officer Peterson OR Chris Hyman any reason to celebrate my return to FCI Tucson. I understand Chris Hyman´s disappointment, it ruined his Batting average, but why would it be that my PO is also a little pissy about it?

Why in the hell would it matter to her?

In fact, aren't we the reason she has a job??? Ah well... I probably had been the one Parolee too many for He/She/It's workload.

Letting my therapeutic inhale/exhale take hold I headed off to catch a bus over to where I had spotted a Real Estate office that specialized in Rental Properties.

As I entered an impeccably dressed woman looked up from her desk when she heard the tinkle of the door-bell…

"Good Morning Sir… how may I help you this morning?"

WOW… What a difference from the last office I had been in. Officer Peterson should take a few lessons from this lady.

"I would like to see what you may have available for Rent"
"Very well... if you have the time this morning would you care to fill out one of our Client Information Forms?"
"I do and I would"

She smiled, revealing a whole bunch of store bought Super Sheen Pearly Whites. As I got busy on the form, Pearly Whites introduced herself… Vicki Long. In just under 2 minutes I knew that she had been born and raised in Tucson, was also the High School Queen at the Home Coming.

She married the King … they are divorced now, but it is OK with her because he drank a lot, she doesn't go out much because most of the guys in Tucson are bums… blah-blah-bla.

Vicki was not the confidant you want to have recently shared a secret with.

As I neared the last question Vicki slid a three inch thick binder in front of me that had obviously been put together with much thought and even more care.

The front cover of the leather notebook touting… "Tucson's Premier Rental Properties".

I sure hope that these Premier Properties have not so Premier rental rates.

I handed her the form and opened the binder. Wow, maybe I should have shared a little autobiography of my own. I think she needs to learn how to qualify; these are way out of my League.

"Ok now... I see here that you work for Precision Chevrolet. That's a nice place, that's where my husband... I mean my X buys his cars. Oh! You've been there for under one month, well that's alright, we all change jobs to move up the ol' ladder. Your previous employer was Precision Chevrolet ... well how is that? Did you just get your dates mixed up? I remember one time my husband I mean my X"

I just couldn't take another trip down memory lane...

"I believe you will see the explanation in the Additional Information section"
"Oh... well then you must have taken time off to enjoy life a little, you know I have always wanted to do.... Oh! OH! OHHH! MY LORD!!"

I'm guessing that she made it to the Additional Information section.

She had her hand covering her mouth trying to stifle the screech, then lowered it to tightly cinch the lapel on her blouse that had been revealing a rather impressive cleavinsky.

Her eyes dropped to the leather bound binder in horror.

Noticing her inability to speak, I'll bet her X would have liked to know that THIS is all it took...

"Look, obviously these properties are not in my range. Would you have something in the range of maybe $500 - $700 per month?"

She couldn't take her eyes off the Binder, as if in my possession the properties were experiencing rapid devaluation.

… "Well… Well… Uh.. I don't know… Uh…. Maybe… Um….."
"Thank you for your time, if I can't find what I'm looking for I may come back to see if you have found anything for me."
"OH!!... um….well…uh, I'm not um… oh!"

I thought it best to leave so she could recover her speaking abilities and hopefully re-iron her lapels.

Maybe I need to re-think about exactly what I am divulging on the next Additional Information section.

I had promised Tim and Joan that I would know approximately how much financial help I would be needing and that I would call them this evening. It was still early enough that I could make another stop. I wanted out of the Peterson House as rapidly as possible. It would be one less thing she could grind me about.

There was an old friend that has been in Real Estate here since they had Dinosaur pens in every backyard, so I gave her a call…

"Billie, how are you… You sexy little thing"
"WHO IS THIS DAMN IT?"
"Someone that has missed you for many years and has come back into your life with intentions of matrimony on his mind"
"You better tell me who this is or I'll be hang'n up on ya"

What a warm and fuzzy feeling it was to hear that sassy ol'drawl again. Billie Jean was THEE undisputed Elder/Mayor/Governor and anything else she set her druthers to in Tucson.

If I was 110 years old, I would ask Billie Jean to be my Bride.

Her family were among the first to settle the desert wilderness of Arizona.

As the story goes… Billy Bob Adam and Bobby Sue Eve were Billie's Great Greats. Her family was responsible for planting the first cactus in Arizona.

I had met her at a Benefit for a Children's Home that she was sponsoring. We hit it off, becoming good friends. Afterwards, throughout the years, I had the esteemed honor of being her escort at various functions.

"Billie, it's Scotty… Scotty Frieze"

"OOOH!! MY LORDIE… Is this really you??"

"Yah, Billie… it's really me"

"Are you call'n me from… from… you know…THERE?"

"No Kid, I'm free again"

"Well now, I know it's you fur sure, nobody else calls me Kid, it sure warms my heart to hear it again."

At one of the functions that I had seen her at she had gotten pretty upset about somebody not doing something.

I told her that she was acting like a little Kid about it. She liked that I admonished her for throwing a tantrum…

"Everybody else is too afraid to say what they're think'n, that's what I like about you Scotty… you ain't scared a me"

The name stuck.

"Daaamn Kid, I sure have missed you"

"You too… I thought you moved away on me without say'n noth'n until I heard what you done. Scott Frieze, why didn't you tell me you needed money, you know I would'a got ya some, you know I got plenty"

"No kid … it wasn't like that. I'll explain it all to you when I see you… soon I hope. Right now I need a place to live and I thought you might know where there is a small place for me to rent, you know, something about $500-$600 a month."

"Ta hell with that... yur move'n to the Ranch"

That is EXACTLY what I would like to do... re-group in the peaceful setting of her sprawling ranch.

The first brick was leveled in the mid-1800's and has been meticulously added on to throughout the years, finally boasting a little over 20,000 sq ft under roof. Nobody seemed to know for sure and Billie wouldn't say exactly how much Ranch land there was... 60,000+ acres was the common estimate. It has been featured in many Homes of the Southwest magazine articles and had been the setting in a couple of movies.

"Ah Kid, there is nothing I would like better, but I just can't, I'm not allowed to move that far out of town and I need to be accessible twenty four seven."
"Well I don't know what yer talk'n about with all that accessible gibberish... I thought you told me that you were free."
"Billie, my freedom has addendums... I'll explain when I see you"
"It must be sumpthin' important cause you only call me Billie when you go an' git serious on me..... What ya need?"

After explaining what I needed she asked for a moment. She came back on the line and gave me an address...

"If you can, hike up yer britches and git on over there, they'll be alook'n for ya"

After hanging up I felt a deep pang in my chest.

Man... if I was only 110 years old.

Just hearing Billie´s voice again gave me a blast of energy, renewed confidence that all will be fine ... forward Ho!!

I glanced at my watch... 3:20.

I will have to pass very near the address Billie gave me, if I haul ass I can make it back to the House before 5.

Located in the Historical District was this six-plex with huge floor to ceiling roll-out arch windows. The meticulous landscaping, lush with every shade of green, various reds and every other color in an Artist's sling framed this Turn of the Century masterpiece. I had to double-check the address.

Billie, I said $500-$600... not $5,000-$6,000.

There is no doubt that this would be a featured Property in Vicki blah-blah Longs leather binder.

I'm here, might as well see if I wrote down the address correctly.

As I started up the walkway the dark well polished door that was framing etched crystal opened. I was greeted by a exquisitely dressed elder Lady that looked like she was the very person that has been greeting visitors since the buildings first day of occupancy...

"You must be Mr. Frieze, I am Lillian Cooper, Madame Larson told me to expect you"

God damn Billie, what did you get me into... you wonderful Crazy Old Broad.

"We have two units that aren't occupied, Madame Larson likes to keep one available at all times... in case she has unexpected guests. She has asked me to prepare for you the larger of the two, please follow me"

We stepped into a middle courtyard which almost put the front yards to shame.

I'm talking a Museum Quality botanical garden.

She opened an etched crystal door and invited me into an impeccably furnished one bedroom that was probably larger than most two bedroom homes.

I didn't need to go in any further...

"Ms. Cooper, I believe Billie... excuse me, Madame Larson misunderstood my need.
"This is an unbelievably beautiful building, however I am not in a position to afford this at this time. Thank you for inviting me in. I will call her to let her know that you were very cordial."

I turned to leave ...

"Excuse me Mr. Frieze, Madame Larson told me that you might say that. This cottage would only require $500 per month and that would also be sufficient to cover all of the utility fees"

I stood there looking at her waiting for some sort of expression that the moment warranted. This cottage had to be no less than $3.000 a month and that would NOT include utility fees.

No facial movement, not even a twitch.

I would hate to play poker with this lady, she was good at her job... very good.

... "Ms. Cooper, this is much larger than I would need and it is very kind that Billie has made this available to me, but I must decline."
"Mr. Frieze, we also have a Casita on the property that is about half of the size of this. I believe Madame will be unsettled with me for not offering to show you that also"

I have seen Billie when she was unsettled with someone. I wouldn't want to be responsible for bestowing that upon Ms. Cooper.

"Alright Ms. Cooper, however we need to do this rapidly, I have an appointment at five that I cannot be late for."
"It is right this way and please... call me Lily"

Obviously relieved that see avoided a confrontation with an unsettled boss, she led the way.

Towards the back of the property was a small one bedroom Casita that was detached from the rest of the property and had it's own entrance from the street. Most likely the caretakers quarters from a by-gone era. It was about half the size as promised and also tastefully furnished.

This just may work.

I glanced at my watch, 4:40.

Holy crap, if that bus is late I'm screwed. Maybe I can make it back on time if I run.

"Ms. Cooper... Lily, thank you for showing me your beautiful homes, these grounds are magnificent, however I just noticed that I am a bit behind schedule. I do need to run, I'll be in touch"

I am sure she didn't know I meant that literally.

The evening manager... Prison guard, was just closing the iron gate at the entrance when I arrived looking like a ball of sweat and severely out of breath. I looked at my watch... 5:04.

"You are late Inmate Frieze, which is a violation of your Parole"

I was so out of breath I couldn't speak, he stood there looking down at me and I, from a considerably lower position with my hands on my knees, just staring up at him. I was ready to pass the hell out.

"You are lucky that I am a little late in locking up… if you tell anyone I did this for you I'll have your ass. Hurry up and get in here God damn it"

That was cutting it too close. I almost provided a perfect reason for Officer Patricia Peterson to claim violation of my Parole. I can not give her justification in sending me back to prison.

During my shower and all through dinner I thought about how nice it would be to call that Casita my home. The larger 1 bedroom was out, there is no way that my PO would approve that when I tell her I am only paying $500 per month. She will know that someone is subsidizing the true cost and that is a violation of my Parole. They would automatically assume drug money or money acquired from ill-gotten gains is involved. They'll never believe it was a gesture from a wonderful Human being. That's unheard of in their world as well as the world that encumbers their work.

Now… that Casita is a little different of a story.

I had told Gary a little about the very tight leash Officer Peterson had me on and about my having to go in the mornings if summoned. I hoped they would lighten up in the future, but couldn't guarantee they would. He said it was great to have me back and that they understand what I'm going through. They have hired employees in the past that were on Parole and they knew the drill.

All he had said to me was…

"When you're scheduled in just get here as soon as possible"

I called Tim and Joan. I filled them in on the happenings of the day and asked if they would wire me enough money to secure the Casita and to pay off my debt for staying in the Observation House. I would pay them back with my first paycheck.

Of course they agreed to help..

… "Scotty, before you worry about paying us back, make sure you have a little money in the bank for emergencies... Oh!! Sorry… are you ok to use banks?"

My sister is the greatest. She has always brimmed with innocence.

"Well Joanie, that's a great question, one that I have been contemplating for quite a while and I don't think I will, I just don't have the confidence any longer that they are able to secure my money like they used to"
"Scott, you don't know that they are insured by the govern…. ah, you're kidding me aren't you, you know that already… don't you?? Scott, don't you??? Scott Andrew… ANSWER ME!!!"
"Good night beautiful Joanie… I love you"

With that accomplished I hit the bed like a sack of potatoes and woke to my alarm seven hours later… in the exact same position as when I entered.

When I arrived at my PO's office I felt better than I had in years, I made it through my eight years of incarceration relatively unscathed and am now back on track. In the last three days I have started a new job with which I made enough to get my own home again. All that is left is to look forward with optimism and not let the past influence my future.

If my PO wants to continue insisting that my past IS my present, she may do so. She can't force me to carry it within, at least not past the doors of this building.

… "Mr. Frieze… Officer Peterson's office through the door"

Life is getting better… 8:40 am!!!

"Good morning"

She just looked at me…

"Sit down"

Well, I will say one thing for her, she is consistent… 100% asshole.

Please dear Lord, can I just knock her out just once… please, please, pretty please. I promise it will be good for her… please.

… "When you signed your copy of the Rules and Regulations document you were not only acknowledging receipt, your were acknowledging that you have read and have accepted its terms and conditions"

I don't know where she is going with this, but I'm getting very uncomfortable.

… "Upon interviewing your Supervisor at Precision Chevrolet I discovered that you did not; either read or did not understand the Provisions regarding the disclosure of the restrictions placed upon you and how they may affect your place of employment"
"My Supervisor, Mr. Gary Patton, is an old friend and he knows everything about me. He understands that I am on Probation and knows how it may affect my work. He has been told that if you require me to be here, I must be here, no matter what my schedule is at work."

"Well he seemed a little surprised when I informed him on exactly how your Intense Probation status may affect your place of employment. If he is willing to accept you, with all that you will be bringing, I will approve your working there"

She chuckled...

"We'll just see how far a good friend will go to back you"

It was a chuckle that puckered me a bit...

"I have found a place to rent, here is the form with all the information. My brother and sister have agreed to help me financially, so I will also be able to pay my fees for staying at the Observation House"
"Pay your new rent and pay your delinquent charges. Just when did I approve your family sending money. Who do you think you are accepting money without my approving it???"
"I haven't and I won't without your approval... OFFICER PETERSON, here is that form... already filled out"

Just one punch... PLEASE.

I felt myself wanting to scream at her in retaliation for her obvious desire to push me to my limit. Scotty... chill bro.... that's exactly what she wants.

... "I won't need to take a look at what you are submitting until you confirm that you do in fact have a job. I have my doubts. Now go pee and report back here tomorrow 8 am"

I found myself running to the bus stop.

What is she talking about... IF I still have a job?? Gary knows I'm on Parole, what it entails. He's hired people in the past under Federal Probation restrictions.

As I waited for the bus to arrive I calmed a bit, she's just trying to fuck with me. Scott… remember; don't take her with you past the doors of her office.

The normal "It's about time Prima Donna" or "Oh!! So you finally decided to come in" was missing from the guys on the front lines.

I didn't like what I was feeling. After only three days the troops had made me feel welcome, especially after trumping Gary at my first meeting on his Tell us about yourself request. Christi, the super beautiful receptionist greeted me with her trademark "Howdy Cowboy", but it fell short.

She seemed nervous, not Christi…

"Gary asked me to let him know when you came in. Give me a sec, let me see if he's in his office"
"Scott Frieze is here, yes sir, I'll tell him. Gary asked if you would please come up to his office"

As I walked down the hall towards my boss's office I could see him at his desk. He was speaking to someone seated out of my view. As I neared the door he stopped talking…

"Come on in Scott, grab a chair… you know Duane Nichols"

Do I ever, the CEO/Owner of Precision Chevrolet, if he is present there is something mighty important going on and by the feel in the room it's not something good.

… "Hello Duane, it's nice to see you again"
"Hello Scott, I'm glad to see you made it through your ordeal and are back into the mainstream again. I have heard a little about what you had done and although I don't quite understand the necessity for your actions I will not judge. From what Gary has been telling me you aren't quite out of the woods yet. I can only wish you the best of luck"

He stood, excusing himself for the next meeting on his agenda…

"I'll let Gary explain our position after our being paid a visit from your Parole Officer"

Gary walked Mr. Nichols to the door and after a brief whispered conversation he returned to his desk…

"Scott, an Officer Patricia Peterson dropped by yesterday, complete with two accompanying Marshals. They arrived in three separate vehicles and made quite a spectacle of themselves. The manner in which they pulled up gave the impression that a raid was taking place which created consternation among the customers and salespeople alike. It was quite a scene, as you can imagine"

I knew what was coming and could only sit there, hands clasped in my lap, picturing the scene.

"Officer Peterson then informed me that this would be the manner in which you will be apprehended, placed in handcuffs and marched out of here for questioning. Whether you are with clients or not, should a bank be robbed in Tucson or Phoenix"

We just looked at each other for a moment.

"She went on to say that this would also take place should they want you to come in for a random urinalysis or just to see if you are at your job… probably at least once a month"
"I don't know what to say Gary. I didn't think she would go to this extent. She WANTS me to fail."
"Well Scott… she is obviously hell bent on not having you work here. She did a good job at scaring us. Duane and I discussed this at length and we cannot jeopardize our reputation or allow this to interfere with the normal course of business. Scotty… we go way back, this is really painful… however…"

"Gary, no need to go on… I understand completely. Please tell Duane that I thank him for allowing me to come back. I am the one that made this bed… I've got to lay in it"

"Scott… if there is anything we can do to help you get past this process let us know, you will always be family"

I left the Dealership without any fanfare… no good-byes. It was hard enough to keep my composure in Gary's office, any questions as to what had happened by my fellow employees and friends just might have broken me down.

I was devastated… a call to Trevor would come later.

After walking a couple of blocks I came upon a little park. I took off my tie, loosened my collar and sat under a tree.

What the FUCK.

I'm gonna tell that fucking bitch what I think of her.

What gives her the right to do this to me?

She wants me back in Prison… I'll give her a MOTHER FUCKING REASON.

I crossed the street and headed for the bus stop that will take me uptown to that He/She/It office. I'm going to explain real well to that BITCH exactly what the FUCK is up.

When I heard the bus driver say "Federal Courthouse Buildings" I jumped up and exited with a distinct purpose. My jaws were clenched, my hands were balled up into fists and I was pissed off. Just as I arrived at the doors there were Marshals clearing a path, escorting a group of orange clad Detainees over to a bus emblazoned with FEDERAL BUREAU OF CORRECTIONS.

As they passed I looked into each guys face and saw that ever recognizable hopelessness. I know that feeling and I don't want that feeling ever again. GOD DAAAAAMN IT…. FUUUUUUUUUUCK.

I spun around on my heels and headed back to the House.

I need to think this through.

Officer Peterson wants me to fail. You can't fail Scott… you CAN'T let her win.

As I entered the dining area, better known as the Chow Hall, I saw Lupita monitoring a half dozen bubbling pots while cleaning and scrubbing another half dozen. She looked up…

"Oh!! Señor Scoot, estas temprano… you early."

She would say something in Spanish, then try to say it again in English….

"I'm soon Americana, necesito talk Americana… no?"

She would then break out with a huge golden smile that confirmed her Origins and dentist were from somewhere very far to the South. I liked her.

She was simple, happy.

Her husband would pick her up in the evenings. She would always go to the driver's side of the truck, open the door, kiss him on the cheek and then proceed to hip check him over to the passenger side as she took over the driving responsibilities. I'm not sure if she didn't like the way he drove or he liked to imbibe a little. It didn't seem to have mattered, there would always be two great big golden smiles driving off down the road.

"Hola, Lupita... tienes poquito café, por favor"

I liked to practice my Spanish whenever I could, hoping I would need it someday. I think Lupita liked me because I was always trying to speak Spanish, maybe because I was the only guy that picked up his plate and cleaned my area after a meal.

She always gave me a little extra on the portions.

"Te vez triste, Señor Scoot, todo esta bien? You OK?"
"Si Lupita... sola mala noticia"
"Pues... necesitas hablar con Dios... El Señor will help you"
"Gracias Lupita, necesito pensar"

After spending the afternoon commiserating, I came up with a plan of action.

I WILL continue forward with my plans to move into the Casita and

I WILL find a job that will tolerate my supervision.

As soon as I walked through the threshold of her office the next morning...

"Well Mr. Frieze, I have been informed as to your being fired already. You see what happens when you decide that you know best and don't follow the Guidelines"

The clock showed 8:15 am, the earliest I have ever been called in.

I believe she couldn't stand to wait any longer to see what my reaction would be to her most recent attempt to piss me off, hoping that I would react in such a way that she could justify sending me back to FCI Tucson.

I took a chair before she could command me to "SIT."

We both sat for a moment just looking at each other.

She had a smirk on her face that got my jaw bones pulsating.

I looked away, took a deep breath and then counted to 5, very slowly...

"Officer Peterson... I thought that I complied with the Provision stating that I must inform my employer regarding my being a Parolee and all that it entails, is it really necessary that it appears that there is a raid being conducted at my work should you want to see me? I lost my job because you pulled up like all hell was breaking loose"
"First of all INMATE Frieze, you don't concern yourself with how I do my job and more-so... actually confronting me on how I carry out my duties. You DO need to concern yourself with finding a job and finding one soon. I have been exceedingly patient with you and your response to my leniency is always argumentative. This entire conversation is going to be noted in your file and I will not fail to mention the combative manner in which you have entered my office this morning"

"I am really trying to do everything by the book, maybe my frustration is appearing combative to you, it is certainly not my disposition, that would be mighty stupid of me, I fully understand that with the stroke of your pen I'm back at FCI Tucson. It is going to be extremely difficult to get a good job if you are going to go in after I'm hired and scare my new employer half to death. How am I to find an employer that is willing to subject himself and his business to... well, I'll use my last employers exact words "We thought there was a raid, so did our customers"

"If you REALLY want to find these employers that are willing to hire Felons such as yourself I suggest FIRST; that you get rid of your bad attitude and SECOND; bring a pen and piece of paper, there is a bulletin board on the wall as you exit. Apparently it isn't positioned well enough to have caught your attention, so I'll be happy to point it out to you if need be. It has a lot of job offers for Felons on Parole. In fact, we get calls every day from these employers telling us that they'll accept the worst we've got just to fill these positions You certainly fall into that category."

"Officer Peterson, I have looked at that board numerous times and all it has to offer is positions for Dishwashers or Gardner Helpers. I'm 50 years old and am really trying to find something that may allow me a chance at having some kind of future"

"I've got a news flash for you Inmate Frieze... THAT is EXACTLY what you will be doing for the rest of your life. You saw how far your ex-employer... excuse me... your GOOD FRIEND, will go to stand behind you. The sooner you accept what your Life of crime has left you with, the sooner we will not have to have these daily BULL-SHIT conversations. Go pee, I've got work to do"

I felt myself shaking as I stood and couldn't even speak... until I got to the door...

"Is it necessary to keep calling me Inmate Frieze? I am trying to get back into society and forget the past eight years... you just keep placing me back in Prison. As far as my "Life of crime", maybe if you read my file you will find out that I haven't spent my life committing crimes"

"Mr. Hy….."

She had a definite "Deer in the Headlights" moment, then quickly recovered…

"Again you step out of your boundaries. I have been sufficiently informed and know exactly who you are and what you have done. Now, once more, I am busy, you are dismissed INMATE Frieze"

Did I REALLY hear her start to say Mr. Hyman??? I've had this nagging voice in my head that keeps telling me that, in some way, Mr. Christopher Hyman is behind the manner in which I am being treated. Officer Patricia Peterson, alias He/She/it, is in charge of administering Chris Hymans revenge!! Her slip of the tongue certainly brings it into the realm of possibilities.

I'm NOT going back to Prison… especially for reasons of satisfying the ego of one big asshole of a Prosecutor.

Could that prick really be so pissed off about my sentence that he's carried it with him for eight years? If he really has carried the pain of my sentencing with him for this long at least it's comforting to know that he's been a MISERABLE prick.

Since the "Hyman" factor is a possibility, I decided to go straight back to Lupita for a cup of coffee and some serious god-damn ponder.

I am NOT going back.

The golden Buenos dias Señor Scoot, followed by a cup a java and a hug from a 300+ pound beautiful woman was just what the doctor ordered to set my mind straight.

I had slipped in and purchased a palm sized notebook at a store next to my bus stop and now I need to create a plan of action.

The entire afternoon was spent looking at my predicament.

Fresh out of prison, in need of a job and a place to live.
50 yrs old. This house is racking up $40 a day and is a source of
ammunition for He/She/It… my newly acquired Adversary.

Her mission to put me back in Prison - VS - My will not to return…
LET'S ROCK

Sorry... Tab's been paid

Part of the Deal my Attorney made with the Prosecutor Christopher Hyman was that if I would agree to be under Intense Parole for five years after my eight year sentence had been served, he would not appeal the verdict.

My attorney Marcus Guerrero strongly suggested that I agree... I did.

Unbeknownst to me some of the guidelines included;

Any activity outside Parolees home needs to written and approved by Probation Officer 24 hours prior; to include trips to grocery store, haircut, family visits, doctor's appointments etc.

No Internet.

Friends visiting at Parolees home are subject to Personal and Criminal background checks and must be approved in advance.

Any establishment that has alcohol is forbidden.

Travel time to approved activity must be accurate within ten minutes.

Check-in when leaving for work, arriving at work or leaving to go home from work, times must be accurate within ten minutes.

A phone call to the Probation Department must be made by Parolee upon arrival or departure from approved location.

Parolee will remain at the location the phone call originated until a return call confirmation has been received.

Bottom line... A five year term of vengeance riddled abuse for a butt hurt prick of a Prosecutor.

The hired gun... Officer Patricia Peterson.

As far as I am concerned Judge Howard D. Goldstein handed down my sentence and I paid.

Fuck you two with this ego driven crap, I'm taking my Life back.

With the development of Chris Hyman being involved in my Supervision I had to make sure there were no missteps on my part.. I received approval for my brother and sister giving me financial assistance, allowing me to move into the Casita owned by my old friend Billie Jean Larson.

The motivation behind Officer Peterson's approval of my loan was that I could only have one loan for $3,000 and there will be none other approved.

One of the provisions in my Intense Parole was that a failure to pay rent on the due date is a violation. Without a job she was betting I would run out of money.

The following day I paid Officer Peterson $440 for the Observation House then collected all my belongings that were saved in a mini-storage unit and at 1 pm moved into the Casita. To my complete surprise Annie had saved all my keepsakes; framed photos, artwork, Santa Fe sculptures, Vases etc. , she even had all kitchen items neatly packed.

After putting everything away, a very content Scotty retired at 8 pm, happy to be alive again and ready to find a job the next morning.

At 9 pm there was a loud pounding on my door. When I opened it there stood Patricia and two uniformed officers…

Inmate Frieze, step out and put your hands on the wall… I was frisked.

Standing on my well lit front porch with one officer, Peterson and the other cop went through my home for approximately twenty minutes. I was told I could re-enter and they left.

I walked into a complete disaster. Everything was thrown on the floor, including drawers, bathroom items… mattresses were removed and tossed aside.

Determined, I cleaned up everything and at 1 am I retired once more.

The next day I found another job, however this time at a Non-franchised Dealership which didn't necessarily need to keep a squeaky clean reputation.

Patricia made her visit to Interview my boss, he was disturbed with the prospect of her Raid visits, but didn't fire me.

Officer Peterson continued with the shake downs of my Casita, on some days twice. Four or five hours later, as I would have everything cleaned up and put away, she would return, tossing it again. I had to stare at the ground and mentally take myself away… far away… a beach in Mexico, to tolerate this obvious attempt to provoke me into a tirade. The days I didn't clean up immediately, expecting her to return, she didn't….. very god-damn frustrating. It was almost as if she had a watch on me and knew my every move… even in my home.

After two months of working and cleaning up my home seven or eight times a week, Officer Peterson started to do her shake downs ten minutes before I was to leave for work.

This put a burden on the workforce of a considerably smaller staffed operation.

I was fired after two and a half months. Fortunately, I had been doing well and was able to set aside a small savings by keeping Patricia from knowing about my bonus structure.

At this point I had a mandatory three days a week visit and pee at the PO's office, the days were changed on a regular basis and I had occasional call-in´s...

"I keep telling you, YOU are a Dishwasher or Gardner's helper... the sooner you accept that the sooner we will get along"

I found a job at a Buy here – Pay here car lot.

I worked as the loan officer negotiating with the banks on C & D paper loans. Helping the fine citizens that were credit challenged... you know, the folks that couldn't help not paying on their previous loans. The good thing was that my hours were more flexible and the business didn't have a reputation issue... a raid from my PO would only accomplish the making of ALL the customers, ALL the salesmen and most likely my Boss to run for the hills and hide until the coast was clear... then, business as usual.

A few days into my new job I got home to find a note on my door saying that Ms. Lillian Cooper needed to see me.

I knocked on her door and it was opened by a puffy faced, almost un-recognizable Lily, who informed me that Ms. Billie Jean Larson had passed on, she was with the Lord now.

I sat down, right then and there on her stoop and with my face in my hands I cried... SOBBED.

Lillian tried to invite me in but I couldn't move, I was in complete shock.

I hadn't even spoken to the Kid since that one phone call, hadn't had a chance to thank her... tell her that she was the greatest.

Officer Peterson was reluctant to allow me to go to the Funeral services of my good friend because I was unable to furnish her with a list of everyone that would be in attendance.

She finally relented.

Good thing. I would have gone without permission, Violation be damned.

The services changed me.

Listening about the life of a wonderful Human Being that cared deeply about the world and ALL its creatures for over 97 years, affected me.

I didn't even know she was 97, she didn't look a day over 95. I know Billie saw from above that I wrote that... I can hear her cowgirl chuckle.

God Bless you Kid... don't be giv'n God too much shit.

Three days after the service I moved into a small studio apartment close to my work. I'm not sure if I moved because of my shame, my grief over not seeing and thanking Billie or because I didn't want to allow Officer Patricia Peterson to desecrate the beautiful building that the Kid restored to perfection.

All I know is that I couldn't stay.

I could feel that the passing of Billie shortened my tolerance for my PO's crap.

On a couple of shake downs I almost exploded.

One of those occasions I had invited a young lady over to my apartment named Alexis, someone that I had met at work

Our plans were to have a Bar-B-Q dinner at my place.

I had informed Alexis of my past and she was ok with me giving Officer Peterson her information.

She was approved.

After a great dinner, fantastic conversation and a mutual attraction we ended up in bed. It would be the first time for me in eight and a half years.

The lights hadn't even been out for ten minutes when the pounding started on the front door.

Slipping quickly into my shorts I tried to explain to Alexis what was going on but the pounding got more deliberate and I ran to answer it.

My PO and three officers quickly barged in and immediately went to the partitioned off bed area and told Alexis to rise. I asked that she be allowed to dress and Officer Peterson said that she could only cover herself with the bed sheet.

Placing us both outside under a very bright entrance light, they tossed my house with curious neighbors watching. The bed sheet that Alexis wore didn't contain a high thread count.

They went through Alexis's purse, with no regard to her privacy nor did they return its contents, electing that everything should be scattered on the floor.

Rightfully so, Alexis was petrified. By the time this thirty minute harassment terminated running was not a quick enough option for my date. I never saw her again.

I am quite sure that Officer Peterson had stationed herself in a position down the street to observe my place and choose the optimum time for the intrusion.

Life under the strict guidelines was starting to take its toll.

I was not a happy person.

It even got worse when my PO called me in to inform me that the results of my last urine contribution came back tainted and that I will be monitored even closer.

Patricia Peterson seemed to be getting more disturbed with me, she started turning up the heat as the days and weeks went on. I can only attribute that to my not reacting to her unquestionably provoking treatment. I started to feel that I would be sent back... even if it meant tampering with my urinalysis.

I was cleaner than a new born babe... something's up.

I went to speak with one of the other Parolees PO, in what I thought was confidence, to see if I could change PO´s.

The next morning at my scheduled appointment with Officer Peterson I was met with pure venom and asked if I had a problem with her being my Supervisor. Trusting that PO Officer Hernandez was honorable in his word of confidence Peterson's question threw me totally off guard. I could only succumb to her vengeance and apologize for my ignorant behavior.

How stupid of me not to recognize her being wonderfully tolerant and extremely lenient with me.

The final straw came when I entered my apartment that afternoon and discovered that it had been shaken down. I went into the bathroom and found my favorite framed photo of my daughters on the floor. The photo had been doused with a tube of toothpaste and there was a clear impression of a boot print that had shattered the glass.

A woman sized boot print.

I WAS LIVID, NOW THE GLOVES ARE COMING OFF

I took a chance that Patricia would be satisfied with her days accomplishments and that she would not return. I needed to get on the Internet. I wanted to see if there was some kind of remedy for my problem. I put my TV on and left out my bedroom window. Two blocks away was a small library, an annex to the main library. I asked if they had Internet.

Upon convincing the librarian that I had just moved into the neighborhood and my ID was somewhere packed in a box at home she issued Patrick Peterson, the new resident in the neighborhood, his Library card.

She was accommodating when asked for a quiet corner for research.

Only twice, in the last six months had my PO conducted a shake down between 9 pm and 4 am. One was my first day; the other had been my dinner with Alexis.

I gambled that from 9 – 11 pm, was my window of opportunity.

I went almost every day for two weeks, following various thought processes until I came upon a Federal Law that only applied to the residents of the State of Arizona.

As I read through the nine page document my excitement grew… Person's under The United States Federal Probation Departments Supervision may transfer their Residence to Mexico. I read on… Parolee must have a job complete with address, phone and name of supervisor, residence with phone and must file a written report to The United States Federal Probation Department once a month.

My excitement was quickly extinguished when in the second to the last paragraph on page nine … "Parolee must be a Mexican National with appropriate documentation".

I continued going to the Library, however not on a daily basis. Officer Peterson had been angrier than usual, stepping up the visits to my home and started mentioning that Parolees have been known to try to hide drug use with cleansing agents and said that my samples have appeared to have been tampered with.

She claimed that it was necessary to document this in my file and to note that the suspicion has been brought to my attention and discussed.

My participation in the discussion was brief…

"Not possible Officer Peterson"

The reply was always…

"I certainly hope you're not implying that it is something on our end… that would be stupid, why would we want to do that?"

I thought to myself… EXACTLY… WHY?

Every time I did go to the Library I found myself going back to the Law that I had found regarding Mexican Nationals. Re-reading it, again and again, I must have read it 50 times until I finally printed two copies. I didn't know what I was going to do with it, I just wanted it.

As the weeks went on Patricia seemed to be prodding me in every manner possible and I got the overwhelming feeling that my days in society were numbered. I came very close a couple of times to just giving up. I started thinking about just making a run for the border and hope I make it. I couldn't sleep at night. I was ANGRY with co-workers, clients, and the cashier at the grocery store... EVERYONE I encountered.

I couldn't take it anymore.

The following Monday, as I waited to be called into Peterson's office, I had been thinking about what I was going to do if she pushed me too hard today, when I heard her talking to someone just on the other side of the door....

"I got my two week vacation starting at one pm on Friday and my plans are to get as far from these Jerk-offs as possible... no phones, just Redwood trees, peace and quiet. I appreciate you helping me out with my workload, I'll return the favor. I should get through most of it before I leave, but I got a ton of shit to do before Friday"

True to form, when I was finally called to her office, she was curt and insulting, but very brief. I was in a little better of a mood just thinking about not having to see her for two weeks.

After work that day I went home and got the print-outs from under the floor mats in my truck that I had purchased two months prior.

There was a clause that stated that the Parolees Probation Officer had to answer the solicitation for Transfer of Residence within 48 hours.

An idea started to form in my mind.

Patricia is leaving at 1 pm on Friday... for two weeks and she's got a shitload of work to do before she leaves... Hmmmm.

If I can get this law in front of her forty eight hours before she leaves, SHE has to answer it, she can't pass it off to the person that is going to help her. It states that the request must be submitted to and answered by the Parolees designated Supervisor. Maybe if I time this just right she won't have time to read it all, I her say that she was roped. If she gets to the part about being a Mexican National... I'll just claim ignorance. If I act like I am confident that I have this right, maybe I can bluff her.

Hell...it´s worth a shot I was ready to go back to Prison just to get away from her anyway. The only problem is that my next appointment is on Thursday. I need to see her before one in the afternoon on Wednesday.

On Tuesday I asked my boss if I could take Wednesday off.

At eleven on Wednesday I walked into the Probation Department, surprisingly calm.

I'm just going to let fate take its course.

I told the Gal at the caged in reception desk that I needed to see Officer Peterson. She looked in her book and told me that I wasn't scheduled.

"I know, but I have a very important matter I need to discuss with her."

She pressed a couple of digits...

"Inmate Scott Frieze is here and would like to speak with you. Yes, I told him, he said it was important"

To my surprise she buzzed me right in.

When I walked into Officer Peterson's office she was standing looking through stacks of files that covered her entire desk top.

"This had better be important INMATE FRIEZ... you can't just walk in here whenever you feel like it... WHAT IS IT?"

I had the print-out in my hand...

"I want to transfer my Residence and Probation to Mexico"
"What the FU..."
"I have a copy of the law and I am formally requesting the transfer"
"Is this some kind of joke... cuz I'm not laughing. What kind of bullsh..."
"I HAVE THE RIGHT... here is a copy of the Law and it states that you need to give me an answer within 48 hours."
"Right now I have a pressing matter... I WILL DEAL WITH YOU TOMORROW... GET OUT OF MY OFFICE AND SINCE YOU´RE HERE, I WANT A URINE SAMPLE... GET OUT!!"
"I am making the formal request, I'm leaving the Request cover letter and a copy of the Law here with you"
"GET OUT"

I walked in calm.. I exited a nervous wreck.

Well, the ball is rolling now, I sure hope this doesn't land me back in Prison. I truly don't want to return, but I can't take her shake-downs, insults, prodding and most of all her talking to me like I was an absolute piece of shit.
NOT ANY MORE.

I glanced at my watch 7:50 am, I opened the door to the waiting room.

At 8:15 am I was buzzed in.

"I don't know what kind of CRAP you were up to yesterday and if I wasn't so busy I would probably be signing the papers to send you back to where you should've never left. I will be leaving tomorrow for two weeks and when I return YOU will be my first appointment. In the meantime you will be reporting to Officer Rodriguez."

I quickly sat down before she could say "NOW GET OUT"

"Officer Peterson, I made a formal request to you yesterday and left a copy of that law with you. It states that if you don't give me a formal answer within 48 hours YOU have violated MY rights"

It was the first time that I raised my voice without her flying off the handle... progress.

"I left it on your desk"

She just looked at me for a moment then looked at her desk. I could see the corner of the letter sticking out between some files.

I started to lean over to grab it.

"Don't you touch ANYTHING on my desk."

She grabbed it and quickly read my cover letter, guffawed, then flipped to the photo copy.

"Be back here at 7:30 tomorrow morning, I have a lot to do and need to leave early. I am NOT happy that you have dropped this on me."

Needless to say… I didn't sleep that night.

7:15 Friday morning; I walked in, I didn't know how this was going to play out, but I was All in on this hand.

At 7:40 I was called in.

Officer Peterson looked like she had been there all night and only half of her desk was clear of files...

"SIT"

Her bark was a little less ferocious.

"I didn't have time to fully investigate this Law, however I did look it up to see if it is in effect and it is. I don't know where you got it, you're not supposed to be using the Internet, we'll deal with all of this when I return."

She grabbed a folder and opened it.

"I have authorized a ten day travel pass for you to go to Mexico for the purpose of looking for a job and a possible place of Residence"

I was sitting there absolutely stupefied, listening to her words and trying to keep the ARE YOU FUCKING KIDDING ME expression off my face.

HOLY CRAP…. IT WORKED!!!!!!

"I will be back in this office seventeen days from today, YOU will be my first matter of business…. 8 am. NOW, GET OUT"

With letter in hand I ran to the parking lot where I had parked my truck. I had so much adrenaline flowing I wanted to run all the way to Mexico. Holy shit, what do I do now… it worked.

I got home and pulled out a notebook and pen, then read the letter again... she gave me permission to go to Mexico!!!

I started to jot down my plan. I didn't want to move off my couch until 1 pm, the time I knew He/She/it would be on a plane.

It was 10 a.m.,. I laid my head back and closed my eyes.

I jumped off the couch and looked at the clock... 2:20.
By six Saturday morning, I had the truck packed to the gills with my belongings, loaded in by matter of importance; everything else went into mini-storage.

ADIOS.....

I kept looking in the rearview mirror... for what I don't know, but it sure felt like the weight of the world had just been lifted off my shoulders.

I knew that this was just the beginning of who knows what... but I was in control of my future. It was no longer in the hands of some Sadistic Sicko Freak hell bent on putting me back in Prison.

Driving through the border at the town of Tecate was easier than I thought it would be, the gate was up and there was a constant green.

Ah!.. lunch time in small town Mexico... time to eat, not stop cars.

I arrived in Cabo San Lucas two days later and got down to business. In less than three days I had a job and a small home rented.

Before I left Tucson I had printed copies for monthly reporting from the Federal probation site. I decided that Patricia gave me permission to find a job & a place to live in Mexico. It must have been her intension to allow me to move here permanently. I understand that we were going to meet again when she got back, but the only way I could get & keep this job was if I could start immediately.

What could I do?

Sorry it was a little earlier than scheduled Patty, but YOU did give me PERMISSION for that purpose and it was on United States Federal Probation Department stationary with YOUR signature.

I mailed my first Report to Peterson's office with all the correct information… Address, phone #'s, employment, supervisors name, etc.

I will play by the rules… I'm just not going back.

I got settled in with my new job by applying and receiving a 90 day work Visa. I needed a Passport, something I had overlooked… so what the hell, I marched into the American Consulate and filled out an application, I was told that I HAD to have one.

The officer at the Consulate said it would be ready in three to four weeks.

The day was coming and I could feel the inevitable lurking as each day turned to night. There were only two places I went… work and home as I waited for the call.

On a Monday afternoon, around three... exactly sixteen days from the time I left Tucson, I had just finished with work and as I walked up to my front door I could hear my phone ringing. When I opened the door it stopped. As I shut the door it started ringing again.

Only one Person has this phone number.

... "Hola"
"What in the FUCK do you think you are doing?"

I guess she recognized my voice.

"YOU GET YOUR ASS BACK HERE RIGHT NOW.. YOU ARE IN VIOLATION OF YOUR PROBATION, I´M SENDING YOU BACK TO PRISON FOR ALL THAT YOU HAVE PUT ME THROUGH... GET ON THE NEXT PLANE TO PHOENIX, YOU WILL BE MET BY THE MARSHALS. WHO IN THE FUCK DO YOU THINK YOU ARE"

I yelled into the phone....

"HEY!!!".......... "HEEEEEEEY... SHUT UP!!!"

She stopped talking.

"FUCK YOU, YOU FUCKING BITCH... YOU HATE THE WORLD BECAUSE YOU DONT HAVE A DICK... YOU FUCKING C---T ... I'M NOT COMING BACK, YOU FUCKING IGNORANT DYKE... YOU MOTHER FUCKING -"

I had the phone held at arm's length and was screaming for all the shame, indignities and humiliation that she inflicted upon me, using vulgarities that have been rarely utilized in my life.

Spit was flying through the air and running down my chin.

My throat felt like I had swallowed hot charcoal.

I don't know if she stayed on the line or not... I continued to purge all the pent up venom, all the hate.

She had treated me like the lowest form of life, pure feces and rubbed my face in it on a daily basis. I felt as if there wasn't any pride left and I had become a mere shell of the man I used to be.

I yelled into the phone until I couldn't yell anymore, tossed the phone onto the chair and walked into the bathroom.

I didn't recognize the face in the mirror.

Tears were pouring out of my eyes, my face was swollen and there was blood and spit still dribbling off my chin... the front of my shirt was soaked pink. I tried to drink some water but I couldn't swallow.

I laid down in bed, it was 3:50 pm.

The next time I moved was to turn off the alarm... 6 am. The phone was making that, I'm not hung up obnoxious beeping sound, so I stumbled into the living room and connected it.

My throat showed the signs of bruising and I couldn't speak. I looked like I got into a fight. Not being able to call work and not wanting them to see me in my current state I elected to go to my neighbor that I had gotten to know and proceeded to try to make up a story using pen & paper.

"Scott, what happened is your business... what do you want me to do for you?"

His assistance resulted in my getting three days off.

My phone rang non-stop so I lowered the ring to barely audible.

Occasionally I'd answer it...

"Hola"
"I am sending a couple of Marshals down there to pick you up if you're not on the next plane to Arizona... WHO IN THE F-------"
"Pat.... PAT... PAAAAT, SHUT THE FUCK UP AND LISTEN TO ME... I AM NOT COMING BACK... so you'd better send'em all because it'll take that many to get me back to Arizona, YOU GAVE ME PERMISSION, I have your signature on United States Government letterhead giving me permission"
"You tricked me"
"I have no Idea what you're talking about"

CLICK

Carrying around hate for another Human being is not healthy, I've never done that before... in this case I couldn't get rid of it.

The calls went on like this for two weeks.

I was constantly looking over my shoulder.

My work notified me that the Consulate called and my Passport was ready.
An appointment was made for the next day, 1 pm.

With all the calls and crap I was dealing with concerning Patricia I totally forgot about my Passport.

I had convinced myself that this is where Peterson is going to try to nab me.

At 9 am I pulled into the dirt lot across the street. By 10 the lot would be full and I will be well hidden. I chose a spot where I had good visibility to the front and side doors.

There were only two ways in or out of the Consulate and I could see them both. It was already getting pretty hot out for 9 in the morning.

This is going to be a long day.

I had been watching the doors and neighborhood activity for about four hours… nothing seemed questionable, other than me sitting in a hot freak'n black truck for four hours sweating my ass off.

Well they're not inside unless they spent the night, nobody lurking behind trees. I started to meander in that direction, doing a 360 scan every couple of steps. 1:07 pm… they said not to be late..

I yanked open the front door and only succeeded in startling the Consulate dude behind the glass enclosure.

As I walked towards the enclosure I did another 360, I can only imagine what an observer would be thinking.

"I apologize for being late, an emergency... you know. Oh, and about the door thing… I thought it was stuck"

Enough Scotty, you sound like an Idiot…

"Anyway, I'm here. Uh, I leaned forward and kind of whispered… you know… uh… Scott Frieze"

PALEEEZE, nobody better have a video of this.

Twenty minutes later I was jumping into my truck, Visa & Passport in my pocket. I don't know what happened, I'm not supposed to be able to get one, at least I wouldn't have been able to in the States.

I quickly pulled it out of my pocket.

Whew... it IS an American passport.

Someone is look'n out for me.

As the weeks turned into months Patricia's phone calls dwindled until there were none. I tried not to deliberate over the reason, I had spent enough of my life negatively because of her.

I just wanted to move forward.

I was doing very well at my job and I liked my new home town, I was even getting pretty good with the ol' Español.

After another five or six months of, nothing from Patty, I arrived at home from work to find a letter shoved under my door. Just as I was opening my door my neighbor rushed over and said that the Immigration van came to my place....

"These guys looked serious Scott.. they were going around the neighborhood asking if anyone had seen you. What did you do bro, they looked SEEREEEUS"
"Ah... don't worry, I already talked to them. It was a mistake, you know, wrong guy".

I shut the door, grabbed the letter and read it.. Your presence is mandatory at the offices of Instituto Nacional de Migracion upon receipt of this letter.

I looked at the clock 5:10.

They're closed. They'll be back tomorrow morning. I need to think this through.

I've got a feeling I know what this is about.
DAAAMN, I really like my new life.
Great job, great town… a simple, quiet life.

I have even met that little Señorita I had spent so many hours dreaming about when I was in Prison.

We've been getting pretty serious about our relationship. She has a son named David, who is a very sharp kid, kind of reminds me of a kid I once knew named Scotty.

DAMN, I don't want to run. If they are on to me, they will ultimately catch me… DAAAAAAAMN

I have been here for about ten months now. If this is the end, so be it, I regained my dignity and enjoyed ten months of how one's life should be lived.

I am thankful that I was able to have a taste of it again.

I didn't want to grow old and die being monitored and driven to the brink of despair.

Patricia, if you want me so badly, here I come.

I MADE IT, I took my life back, as brief as it may have been, I DID IT.

Officer Patricia Peterson, you will never be able to secrete this from my memory.
I will continue to live this in my minds eye until the last shovel of dirt hits my chest.

I left my house at 6 am and went to my favorite breakfast spot. I didn't want the van to show up and haul me away.

I'm going to walk into the Immigration office with my head held high, dignity intact and face the music.

I pulled in at 8:15, exited the truck and without pausing, walked in, handed the Officer seated at the desk my letter and said …

"I am Scott Frieze."

He stood up immediately, asked me to follow him and we were buzzed through a door.

The sound gave me the chills.

Upon entering a hallway there was a rather LARGE gentleman, in uniform, walking towards us.

He introduced himself and asked me to please step into his office.

I quickly looked around to see if I could locate an avenue for escape, should one be desired.

I introduced myself and offered my hand in greeting, he returned the gesture by shaking my hand in his skillet sized ham hock.

Whoa… big dude.

Just as I was regaining my seat the door opened, then closed.

I felt someone behind me, I turned to see two EXTREMELY large fellows standing behind my chair.

Whoa… two bigger dudes.

Just my luck, the three biggest Mexicans in Mexico.

My avenue for escape that I had located should it be desired, has just been eliminated.

"Señor Frieze, I need to ask you a couple of questions regarding your leaving the United States of America and also your application for Permanent Residency here in Mexico. Is that alright with you and you will be truthful?"
"Yes that is ok with me and yes, I will be truthful"

My first impression was that I liked this big dude, he had a good manner about him and Señor Columbo also knew the truthful answer to every one of his questions. We should get along, I had already planned on telling the truth.

"First, I would like to ask you if you have ever had any problems with the law, you know, like committed any crimes?"

Big dude doesn't need to warm up… he just starts with a fast ball.

"Yes sir, I have"
"And what would that crime or crimes have been?"

I'm a warm up kind of guy…

"I have committed a couple normal petty crimes like many youths have during the course of their teenage years, you know… when we are trying to decipher the difference between Stupid and Reasonable behavior."

I think I lost big dude on that one, alright, I've broken a sweat...

"I believe what you are asking me is have I committed any serious crimes in my life and the answer to that is… Yes sir, I have"

"And what would that be?"
"Bank Robbery"

We were looking dead straight into each others eyes. Not to play stare-down or tough guy… just plain straight talk. I believe we wanted the other to know it was frank and it was honest.

I could see in his eyes that he had expected me to try lying, dance around the truth, maybe half-truths to just get by so I could get the hell out of there.

"Did you spend time in the Carcel, Cereso… excuse me, is the correct word jail.?"
"Yes sir, I spent eight years in Prison and after serving my time I was to be under Probation for five years."
"You are saying that you completed ALL of the eight years and that they let you out?"
"Yes sir... I did and yes... they did"

He kind of chuckled, I think my answer registered as funny in the manner it was delivered. He looked up at two bigger dudes, got rid of his smile and returned to the serious matter at hand.

He started thumbing through the file in front of him, read something and said once more..

"You served ALL the time that the Judge gave you and then they opened the door and told you to leave?"

They didn't need to say anything to me, just show me a crack in that freak'n door.

"Yes sir, that is correct"

He looked perplexed...

"Alright... Now, on the application you marked the box that said you have never had a Felony... No?"

"Yes, I marked that I have never had a felony, that is correct"

"But you just now told me that you do.. I think Bank Robbery is classified as a Felony... No?"

"That is correct... it is a Felony"

"Did you know that giving the Gobierno de Mexico false information is against the law and you could be in put in Jail here for that?"

"I would guess that the Gobierno de Mexico wouldn't be too pleased about someone lying on the application"

"But you did"

"Yes sir, I did"

"Why Señor?"

"Well my reason is pretty simple... if I didn't you would not have let me in"

We were still looking at each other and I could see that he wanted me to continue, when I didn't elaborate...

"Why did you want to be here so much?"

BAM!!... THAT was the question I was waiting for. I didn't want to just start trying to explain this whole sordid nightmare in fear that he, at some point half way through, would feel that he's heard enough and make his decision on my fate. I wanted to be invited to explain my reason. One thing I had learned about the Mexican culture... once you are invited to do something it would be rude to not allow that person the time needed to his or her satisfaction.

I wanted him to hear my entire story.

"Would you please allow me the time to fully explain my reasons for lying on the application... I would like you to hear the complete reason."

"Certainly Señor, I will give you all the time you need… this is a serious matter"

At this point I believe he had had ample time to discern that I wasn't a danger so he dismissed two bigger dudes.

I touched on "As far back as I can remember.." and told him the highlights of the trial. I explained the manner in which I had been treated after being released from Prison, blow by blow.

It took the better part of two hours.

When I was satisfied that he understood why I made the decision to lie on my application and to the Gobierno de Mexico…

"So here I am"
"Señor Frieze, I will guess that you know why you are here, but let me tell you so there is no question in your mind. I have received a Request to Extradite from Mexico City where an official from your Government has submitted the appropriate paperwork. I am the Official in this area that has the job to approve or deny this order"

I was literally slumped in my chair, the exhaustion and strain from the prior months were taking their toll, I just wanted this all to end.

"There are some parts of what you have told me that I would like to investigate further. There seems to be conflicting information. Did you come here this morning because you found our letter under your door… No?"
"No… I mean Yes"

That double negative way of asking their questions has always thrown me off.

"Señor, one of our vans did not need to pick you up… No?"
"I drove my truck here by myself"

"You are a smart hombre, almost always we have to drive north to one of the Pueblitos and pick up the person that is trying to run... I don't like that... gasolina no es barrata... No?"

I didn't say anything.

"Do you have this letter you are talking about, the one that this person"

He looked down at the notes he had scribbled as I told him the story...

"Officer Patricia Peterson gave you before you drove here?"
"Yes sir, I do"
"Do you have a copy of this letter or just the original?"
"I have several copies"
"I would like to have one of my Officers follow you to your home, may I have one?"
"Absolutely"
"Do you have enough food in your home?"

I didn't know where he was headed with that question , but If he or the two bigger dudes are hungry I don't have enough...

"Yes sir"
"So then if I ask you to go home and stay there, you won't leave for any reason, you will do that... No?"
"Sir, I will not leave my home"
"I believe you. I will tell you when I want to see you again, thank you for coming in"

When I walked outside and started for my truck I noticed a white van parked behind me, with half of two bigger dudes behind the wheel.

Man... I need a long Siesta after that.

Two days later the other Half showed up on my door step and said that his Jefe wanted to see me.

"Señor Frieze… Please sit down"

He appeared to be a little pissed off, well… I tried… I guess I'm going back to Prison.

"Why did you pick Mexico to come to?"
"Well… Besides being the closest place when you want to get the hell out of America fast…"

He didn't laugh.

"The area that I grew up in was predominately Mexican, I grew up eating menudo on Sundays, I just want to live a quiet, simple life where I can live out my years in peace"

A real uncomfortable silence was going on…

"When I called to speak with Officer Peterson to find out if what you told me is correct she told me that she didn't have time to speak with me and that I just need to put you on a plane to Phoenix where the Marshals are waiting or she will speak with my boss in Mexico City and I won't have a job tomorrow"

He just sat there for a moment studying my face.

"I am afraid that my boss, Señor Presidente, is very busy and will not have the time speak with HER, it takes many hours in the day to run a country, no?"

With that he opened a file that was on the corner of his desk and removed two official looking documents and my Visa. He had a huge smile on his face when our eyes met once more. He then grabbed a mallet sized rubber stamp, flipped open a tin containing ink and without removing his smile or breaking our eye contact.

THWACK - THUD
THWACK - THUD
THWACK – THUD

……………. "BIENVENIDO A MEXICO SEÑOR FRIEZE"

farewell my pearl

reason for being

I shall be

Vacant of reason

tc   tam

Thanks
Jungle Jim
Alfonso Gasio G
Vagabundos del Mar

The other five in the finest six-pack of siblings

A Special thank you to
Don Watson... without the Blue Moon factor
this would never have been

Marcus Pomeroy, your friendship & support has been and always will be
invaluable

Thanks to the readers Scotty will be able to file the
SSIIJ6Y plan under the heading "Completed"